GCSE Home Economics

TEXTILES FOR PEOPLE

Maureen Wilkinson

Longman

The books in this series

Families and Child Development by Sharon Goodyer
Food for Health by Dodie Roe
Home and Consumer by Dodie Roe

The following topics relevant to this book are covered
in other titles in the series.

Families and Child Development
Clothes
Toys
XYZ

Home and Consumer
Consumer information
Consumer protection
Furnishings
Labelling
Stain removal
Washing

Longman Group UK Limited
*Longman House, Burnt Mill, Harlow, Essex, CM20 2JE, England
and Associated Companies throughout the World.*

First published 1988
ISBN 0 582 22476 4

Set in 10/12 point Palatino and Univers Linotron
Printed in Great Britain
by Hazell, Watson & Viney Limited, Aylesbury

Contents

Preface

This book is one of a series of four, written particularly to help teachers interpret and pupils succeed in the GCSE examination courses in Home Economics. The authors have worked together on developing a problem-solving approach and have tried out ideas in the classroom. The other books in the series are:

Families and Child Development
Food for Health
Home and Consumer

What is so special about this examination?
One of the aims of the GCSE examination course is to develop the skills of decision making, which are necessary throughout life. It also aims to help individuals to lead effective lives as members of the family and community, and to provide them with the management skills to use resources wisely and to recognise the interrelationship between the need for food, clothing, shelter, and security.

What does this approach entail?
The authors of these books have used the subject matter of Home Economics to provide pupils with opportunities to:
— identify needs in a particular area;
— recall, seek out, and apply knowledge relevant to the situation;
— identify ways of carrying out a task or solving a problem, isolating the priorities;
— decide upon and plan a course of action;
— carry out a course of action;
— evaluate the effectiveness of the course of action.
It is hoped that if pupils are able to develop decision making skills they will be able to recall and apply these criteria in different situations.

How do these books help with this approach?
The books are written with an alphabetical sequence of topics, similar to a catalogue, not as a course to be followed through from beginning to end. Units of work from within one book, or from across several, can therefore be put together as the teacher wishes. This supports the underlying philosophy of the GCSE course to integrate the four main aspects of Home Economics.

The topics in the catalogue start from the pupils' own knowledge, provide trigger material, practical exercises, discussion points, ideas for visits and speakers, and suggest resources which might be used to extend experience.

Textiles for People complements the information on techniques that is readily available in traditional reference books, and concentrates on features of the subject which are new to GCSE courses.

Dodie Roe
Series editor

About using this book

There are five symbols used in this book:

 means that you have to "collect" something.

 means that you have to "send for" something.

 means that you can find out more information by looking either in another part of this book; or in another book in this series; or in a computer program, leaflet, booklet, or other publication; or by visiting somewhere or asking someone to visit you.

 means that you can try out an activity on whatever you happen to be making in textiles at the time (used in "Colour" topic only).

 means that you should wear safety goggles when carrying out an experiment.

Acknowledgements

We should like to acknowledge the help of the following bodies in reading and correcting the relevant sections of the text: Association for Science Education Laboratory Safeguards Sub-committee, British Man-made Fibres Federation, International Institute for Cotton, International Wool Secretariat, World-wide Butterflies Ltd.

Photograph acknowledgements
We are grateful to the following for permission to reproduce black and white photographs:
Camera Press, pages 2 *above left* (photo: Christer Lundin/IMS), 14 *below left* (photo: Jon Blau), 22 *above* (photo: Stephen Davis), 22 *centre right*, 22 *below right*, 23 *left* (photo: Fionnbar Callanan), 60 *below left* (photo: R. Open), 60 *below right* (photo: Rolf Mader); Sally & Richard Greenhill, pages 2 *below left*, 14 *above left*, 14 *below right*, 42, 162 *above right*, 162 *below right*; ICI Fibres, pages 23 *below right*, 133; International Wool Secretariat, page 92 *below*; Camilla Jessel, pages 1, 2 *above right*, 16, 60 *above left*; The Keystone Collection, page 76; Frank Kitson, page 8 *below*; Luton Town Football & Athletic Co Ltd, page 22 *below centre*; Mothercare, page 162 *below left*; Network, page 2 *below right* (photo: John Cole); Robin Wools, page 60 *above right*; Dr Tony Brain/Science Photo Library, page 87 *above*; Shirley Institute, pages 87 *below left*, 87 *below right*, 88, 92 *above*, 97, 101, 103; Topham Picture Library, page 162 *above left*; Victoria & Albert Museum, page 23 *centre* (photo: Cecil Beaton); Maureen Wilkinson, pages 13, 14 *above right*.

Acknowledgements for colour sections
Page 1: Material provided by London College of Fashion
    2: Material provided by London College of Fashion
    3: Material provided by London College of Fashion
    4: Material provided by London College of Fashion
    5: Material provided by courtesy of Clothkits
    6: *left*   Habitat
       centre   Robin Wools
      below right   Clothkits
    7: *above*   Bruce Coleman (photo Allan Power)

Introduction

When you were born you were naked.

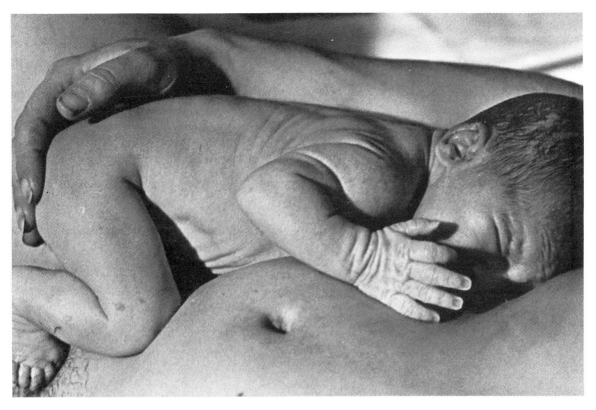

Figure 1

A few seconds later you were wrapped up in a piece of cloth. Ever since then you have been using textiles, and you will go on using them in one way or another for the rest of your life.

When you were a small child, an adult chose everything for you. As you grew older, you began to take an interest in styles and colours. Sometimes you were allowed to help choose things like clothes and bed-covers, but an adult always decided what would be good value for money, and how much to spend.

Now you probably have some money of your own and can decide for yourself how you will spend it.

How much of your money do you spend on things made from textiles? When you are an adult you will spend about 10% of your income on textiles. Unless you are very rich indeed, you will always have to be careful to spend it wisely.

(a) Danny

(b) Mrs James

(c) Myra

(d) Jim

Figure 2

This is a book for people like you, who have to make decisions about textiles. It cannot tell you exactly what to make, or buy, or wear, because everyone who reads a book is different: the right answer for one person could easily be the wrong answer for someone else. Instead, the book aims to help you to make the decisions for yourself.

It will help you:

- to work out what you need, and to make the best use of resources like time, money, materials, equipment and people;
- to decide what information you will need in order to make wise choices;
- to find that information, either here in the book itself, or somewhere else;
- to plan your work so that it goes smoothly;
- to decide for yourself whether your work is good enough.

The book has been arranged like a catalogue, from A to Z, so there is no need to read right through it from beginning to end. But you will probably find it useful to start by reading the next few pages, so you can make the best use of the book in future.

Even something as simple as choosing a pair of socks needs a lot of thought, or planning.

The first thing the people in figure 2 need to think about is who the socks are for, and the job the socks will have to do.

When you are buying, choosing, or making something yourself, you will find it helps if you always think about it in stages.

The next step is to think about the fabric that will do the job best.

Danny	**Mrs James**	**Myra**	**Jim**
Wool is very absorbent, but so is cotton and I think it would be cooler. It can also be washed on a hotter setting than wool. I think cotton with a towelling inside would be best, with perhaps a bit of nylon to make them wear better.	*Not wool – I think it irritates his skin – and anyway his mum might forget and put them in the machine on a hot wash. Possibly cotton, or an acrylic? Not nylon, because it isn't absorbent enough.*	*Definitely pure wool. Dad loves natural fibres, and it'll be beautifully warm for winter. Nylon reinforced heels and toes, perhaps, to make them wear better?*	*I think I'll look for one of those nylon mixtures. That should be reasonably hard-wearing and comfortable. If it's too expensive I'll go for all nylon – I don't suffer from sweaty feet, and I know it'll be very hard-wearing.*

Would it be best to make the socks, or to buy them ready-made?

Much too difficult to make – I can only knit squares.	*I'd rather like to knit them – Ryan's loved all the sweaters I've made for him. And I'd be able to use up all the ends of yarns from the sweaters.*	*I could try. I'm quite good at knitting, though I've never done anything as complicated. I might make a mess of them. And I don't know how long it would take.*	*I'm not wasting my time making something so boring. It would be different if they were going to be fun socks . . . .*

Research – what is available in the shops?

Plenty of choice, from very cheap to very expensive.	*I didn't see anything I liked. They were either too expensive, or horrible colours, or all nylon.*	*I saw a pair Dad would like, but they were awfully expensive. I'll find out if it would be cheaper to make them myself.*	*Not a bad selection. I don't think I'll have any problem getting something.*

The final decision

Danny

I bought these in the market. Dirt cheap – an absolute bargain.

Mrs James

I'm going to knit them myself. I've bought a pattern, and I've got the right sized needles at home. I've got to sort through my oddments of yarn. Apart from the colours, I've to make sure they're all the same thickness, and made of fibres that will wash and wear the same.

Myra

By the time I've bought the yarn, and a pattern, and a set of needles, it would cost nearly as much as ready-made socks. It's not worth the risk. I'll buy the ones I saw yesterday.

Jim

I'm going to buy the dark grey nylon-and-wool ones. They're not as cheap as the pair in the market, but I know that the shop will take them back if they don't wear well.

Last, but very important – looking back and deciding whether the final decision was the right one (*evaluating* the decision).

They went a bit funny after they'd been washed a couple of times: the feet stretched and went baggy where the towelling is. Next time I think I'll pay more and get a better pair. I've learned something about value for money.

Yes, I'm very pleased with them. Ryan loves them, and they're wearing and washing very well. I think they could have been a bit longer – next time I'll measure his leg length as well as his foot size.

They're a great success. Dad wears them a lot and was really pleased I'd remembered how he hates socks that are too short. I'm going to have a go at making a pair as well, though, just to find out if I can.

I think I made what they call "a wise buy". They're comfortable, they wash and dry easily, and so far they're wearing well. (And nobody's noticed them at work, so they must be respectable enough.)

How would you set about solving the problems below? What would you think about? What would you need to find out? How would you evaluate what you had done?

Your grand mother loves sitting in the sun in her deckchair. It is getting very shabby, however, and the fabric is beginning to split at the top. You offer to re-cover it for her.

Your little sister is always late for meals, and then complains if her boiled egg is not hot. It is her birthday in a few weeks, so you decide to make her a special egg-cosy for a present.

Your local youth club is having a proper coffee-bar put in. The area they are going to use needs brightening up, so the leader has asked you to make a set of wall-hangings for it.

You are fed up with carrying your sports gear around in a plastic carrier bag. Your mother grumbles about the way the muddy boots make the clothes even filthier.

When you were planning how to solve the problems on page 4, did you think about any of these things?

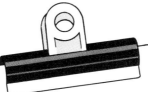

Who is it for? What will they like?
How, where, how often will they use it?
Is this important?
Will it need to be comfortable, strong, windproof, waterproof, or flame-resistant?
Will it get dirty? If so, how? How will it be cleaned and how often?
How long will it have to last? Will it get rubbed, or pulled a lot?
Will it matter if it gets creased? Is safety important?
Will it have to keep warmth in, or heat out?
How big should it be? What shape and colour would be best?
Is fashion important?
Will it have to match something else?
What sort of fabric will be best?
Would it be sensible to make it, or buy it ready-made?
How long will it take to make?
What equipment will be needed, and is it available?
Will a pattern be needed?
If so, can I make it myself, or should I buy one?
How much fabric will it take? Where will I get it from?
Will I need any extras? How shall I make it?
Shall I decorate it? If so, when should I do the decoration?
Will it need loops, pockets, openings, fastenings, or straps?
If so, how big, and what sort, and where?
When should I put them on?
How shall I press the fabric, or neaten off the raw edges, or join it together?
How can I tell whether it is good enough?

Figure 3

These are the sort of questions you will be asking yourself whenever you are using, choosing or making things from textiles. In order to make wise decisions, it is important to ask the right questions.

KEY WORDS
Absorbent soaks up moisture (like water, ink, dye or sweat).
Evaluate to examine what has been done, or what has been made: to decide how good it is, and how it could have been improved.
Reinforced strengthened in some way.
Research gathering information.

Advertising

Collect advertisements, brochures, newspaper and magazine articles about textiles, things made from textiles and textile equipment.
Send for *British advertising code of practice* and *How to complain* from the Advertising Standards Authority (address on page 197).

I never buy things that are heavily advertised - if they have to advertise it, it can't be any good.

Very useful - they help one to keep up-to-date with what's available.

Some of them are fun, aren't they? And they often give you some really good ideas.

Goods and services are advertised in many different ways and many different places. Some of these advertisements have cost a great deal of money; some of them have cost very little. What they all have in common is their aim – to persuade as many people as possible to buy the goods or services.

People often have strong feelings about advertising. What do you think about it? It would be interesting to discuss the subject with some of your friends. As well as saying what you think, try to work out *why* you have those opinions – is it because of your own experiences, or things that have happened to members of your family?

How much have you been influenced by what your friends or family say, or what you have read somewhere, or seen on television?

Whatever you think about it, advertising is a part of today's life that is not going to go away. To be a successful shopper, it helps to understand something about why people advertise, and some of the ways in which they try to persuade you to buy.

When you finish this course you will be able to make some very attractive things. Friends who do not have your skills may well ask you to make something for them. What if you decided to start a business, and make your living by selling the things you make?

On your own, or with a group of friends, think about what you could make that is not already available in the shops (this is known as "finding a gap in the market"). Sketch some ideas and choose the one you think is best. Decide what materials you would use to make it, and work out what it would cost.

If you sold only two items a week, how much extra (on top of the cost of making them) would you need to charge in order to earn a reasonable wage? Do you think people would be prepared to pay this price?

Imagine that you sold 20, or 50, or 100 items a week. How much would you need to charge for each item, in order to earn the same weekly wage? Do you think people would be more likely to buy your product at this price?

But people will not buy your product if they do not know about it. In order to sell more you will have to do two things:

1) Tell people about your product and make them notice it.

2) Make them want it.

One way you could do this would be to get a magazine or newspaper interested in your product, and persuade them to tell their readers about it, like the article in figure 4. This is known as public relations, and has the great advantage of being very cheap. Also, many people will take more notice of what they read in an article like this than if you told them about your product yourself. Look through your collection of magazines and newspapers and collect articles that give this sort of free publicity.

Figure 4

A New Line in Knitwear

A local boy's hobby has proved so popular with friends and neighbours that he has decided to turn it into a business. Nineteen-year-old Alan Greenwood got hooked on knitting when he was a pupil at Ashford Manor School.

"The part I liked best was designing patterns on the machine's punch-cards. Just for fun, I made my girl-friend a sweater with the same pattern as her new tartan jacket. After that, several people asked me if I could copy the pattern on some of their clothes, and soon I found I was spending all my spare time making things for people."

If you think that some custom-made knitwear would put the finishing touch to your favourite outfit, you can find Alan at 5 Ormond Crescent (tel. 06794).

Or you could advertise.

In 1986, it cost £57 000 to advertise on the back cover of the *News of the World* colour magazine, the highest full-colour page advertising rate in Britain.

It can cost more than £172 000 for a single 30-second prime-time slot on all commercial TV channels in the UK during peak weekend viewing hours. Peak weekday evening viewing hours can be even more expensive, at more than £193 000.

How much does advertising cost?

This will depend on the type of advert, and where it is shown. Figure 5 shows some of the main types. Ask the advertising departments of your local newspaper, a national daily, a national Sunday paper, a colour-supplement, a weekly magazine, a monthly magazine and a specialist magazine, how much they charge for different kinds of adverts. If they print in colour, ask how much this costs. (You could telephone or write for this information, or look it up in *British Rate & Data* in your local reference library.) Figure 6 shows another type of advert.

Find out how much it would cost to have leaflets or glossy brochures, such as those shown in figure 7, printed for you. (Look in the Yellow Pages to find local printers.)

Figure 5

Figure 6

Figure 7 A selection of advertising leaflets.

Where should you advertise

You want your advert to be seen by as many people as possible, of course, but they must be the right sort of people, the ones who are most likely to be interested in your product.

Who do you think they are? What do they read? Where else might they see your advert? Would they see your poster, or pick up leaflets or brochures when they went shopping, or to the clinic, or the public library? Or could you reach them by sending leaflets out with the local paper, or by post?

Next time you are out, notice where different firms advertise their products or services.

Look through your collection of magazines and newspapers again. Where do you see most advertisements for these things?

Tools, equipment or materials for different textile crafts
Soft toys
Embroideries, hand-woven goods, macramé
Cheap clothes
Expensive clothes

Way-out fashion
Furnishing fabrics
Dress fabrics
Dressmaking or soft furnishing services
Knitting yarns and patterns

Visit shops where they sell these things and collect examples of leaflets and brochures. How much information do they contain? Are they more, or less interesting than an advert or poster? How helpful do you think they are?

How should you advertise?

Any form of advertising is going to cost money, so you want to be sure that people really notice it. Could a picture do this for you?

Flip casually through some of your magazines. Collect the adverts for clothes, textiles or equipment that use a picture to catch your eye. What was it about each of them that attracted you?

Was it the colours?

Did it surprise, shock, or puzzle you?

Did it make you laugh?

Did it show a "look" that you would like to copy?

Was it a picture of something that you are thinking of buying soon (a piece of craft equipment, perhaps)?

Could words attract people's attention? Flip through your magazines again and see if there are any adverts that use a headline to make you stop and look again. What did the headline say that made you notice it?

Will the picture or the headline be enough, or will you need to give your customers more information about your product? If so, what will you say to make people want to buy it? Why should they want to buy yours, rather than someone else's? Of course, you will mention its good points, but will that be enough?

If you choose your words carefully, you could suggest that by buying your product they will change their lives in some way.

Will it make them feel rich?

> **Superb . . .**
> **ELEGANT . . .**
> **Luxurious . .**

Will it make them a trend-setter?

> *DO YOU DARE? . . .*
> *It takes a real man to . . .*
> *EXCITING . . .*

Will it be much more useful than what they already have?

Does everything you could possibly want . . .

Couldn't be simpler to use . . .

AUTOMATIC . . .

The latest micro-chip technology . . .

Will it make them think they are saving money?

Real value . . .
ONLY £25 . . .
SPECIAL OFFER . . .
For a limited period only . . .

Interest-free credit . . .
Up to 50% off . . .

Will they get something for nothing?

FREE GIFT . . .
Free – hundreds of pages of the latest. . . .

Will it solve a personal problem?

At last – real fashion in your size . . .
Look smoother in ten days . . .
Can help you, too . . .

Collect advertisements that use words like these. Underline (or make a list of) those words. How many of them give real information about the product? Are any of them building up people's hopes or fears in order to make them want the product?

Design some advertising for your own product. If you are working with some friends, each member of the group could design a different type of advert: a poster, a leaflet, a brochure, a full-page advert, something smaller for the local paper.

Before you begin, you will have to agree about your "house style". What sort of lettering will you use? If you have a trade-mark or logo on your labels, should you use this somewhere in the adverts as well?

You will have to be careful that your advertisement conforms to the British Code of Advertising Practice. If someone complained that you had said something dishonest, you could be in serious trouble. Are your advertisements "legal, decent, honest and truthful"?

To find out how effective your advertising is, you need to have a real product to sell. Perhaps, as part of your course-work, you could design and make a product for sale in school. If you cannot do this, you can get some idea of "customer reaction" by displaying your adverts somewhere in your school, and asking pupils, staff and visitors to vote for the one they like best.

Find out whether press (and television) advertising is effective, by playing a game. Collect about 20 advertisements for well-known products and blank out the name of the product. (Typewriter correcting liquid will do the job quickly.) Give each advert a number, pin them up round the room or in the corridor, and ask passers-by to name each product.

Find out if *Which*, or a magazine like *Good Housekeeping* has recently reported on something to do with textiles. If they have, make a note of the products that were tested. Collect some advertisements for those products, and compare them with the report.

SEE ALSO

Rights and responsibilities for information about your rights and responsibilities as a consumer.
Shopping for more about some of the ways in which retailers try to persuade you to buy from them.

See the book *Home and Consumer* (in this series) for information on legal and voluntary controls on advertising.

Children

Collect catalogues and magazines with pictures of children's clothes, toys and furnishings.
Textile items that have been used by children of different ages, for example clothes, towels, bedcovers, soft toys, "comforters", rugs, dressing-up clothes.

How many items made from textiles can you see in Figure 8?

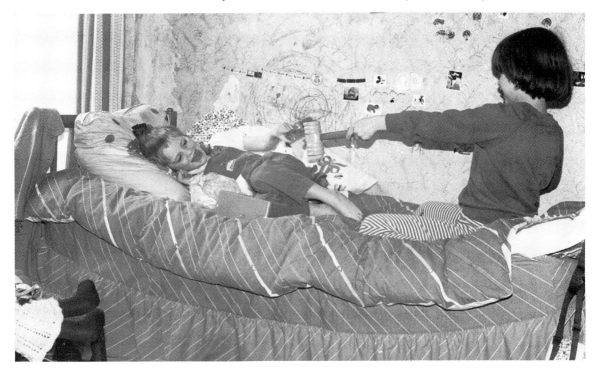

Figure 8

Try to find opportunities to watch children of all ages. Notice what they are doing, what they are playing with, and what they are wearing.

With a small group of your friends, look through your catalogues and magazines and choose a toy, an outfit of clothes, and an item of furnishing for each of the children in Figure 9. How did you decide, when you were making your choices?

Note the points you thought were important, and then look at the checklist on page 15 to see if you had missed out anything, or if you had thought of something that is not on the checklist.

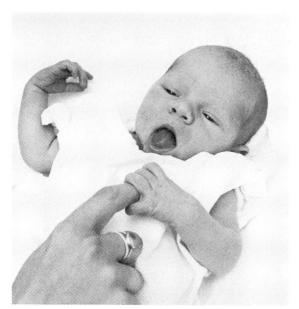

(*a*) *Young baby*

(*b*) *Two-year old*

(*c*) *Five-year old*

Figure 9

(*d*) *Seven-year old*

Checklist for children (in alphabetical order)

Children's needs change as they grow older, so some of these points only apply to children of a certain age: some of them only apply to toys, or to furnishings, or to clothes.

Appearance
- Will the child like it?
- Will he or she look good in it?

Care and maintenance
- How often will it have to be cleaned? (Check: the colour; how, where and how often it will be used; the child who will use it.)
- Is it washable? (Check: hand or machine.)
- Will this be easy? (Check: the weight when wet; the fabric or yarn.)
- Will it have to be ironed? Will this be easy? (Check: awkward gathers; pleats; frills.)
- Will the item need any special care? (Check: the stuffing; the fastenings; the decoration or trimmings; the lining.)

Comfort
- Will any part of it irritate the child's skin? (Check: the fabric or yarn; the way the edges are finished; does the child have a sensitive skin?)
- Will it let the child move about freely? (Check: the fabric – thick or thin, firm or elastic; the size and shape; the weight of the item.)

Durability
- What sort of wear-and-tear will the item get? (Check: the child who will use it.)
- Is the fabric strong enough? (Check: the fibre content; the yarn type; the fabric construction.)
- How well is the item made? (Check: the stitching; the edge-finishes; how strongly are fastenings, decorations or trimmings fixed?)

Growing up
- In a garment, is there any room for growth? (Check: hems; seams; straps; waistbands.)
- If the child is very young – will there be enough room for a nappy?
- Can it be let out, or let down without it showing? (Check: the fabric – will unpicking leave a mark, and will there be a dark shadow if the fabric has faded?)
- If you are making the item yourself, how big will the child be by the time it is finished?
- How long will the child go on liking it? (For example, will he or she still like "teddy bears" in a year's time? See figure 10.)

Figure 10 What might this boy think of the teddy-bear on his sweater?

Learning

● Will the item encourage the child to practise talking and listening? (Check: colours; textures; shapes; stories.)

● Could there be something to count, or sort into sets? (Check: buttons; spots; pockets; animals or trains.)

● Could it help the child to practise new skills, like getting dressed or undressed? (Check: inside and outside, back and front – is it easy to tell the difference? Fastenings – will they be easy to manage? Can the child reach them easily? Openings – are they big enough?)

Play

● Will the item help the child to play his or her favourite games, or to invent new ones? (Check: the child; his or her playmates.)

Protection

● Will the item need to keep the child cool, or warm, or dry, or clean (figure 11)? (Check: when and where it will be used; properties of the materials it is made from; its shape; how it is made.)

Safety

● Is there anything about the item that could harm or injure the child in any way? (Check: materials; fastenings; shape; trimmings; workmanship.)

Figure 11 When babies start trying to feed themselves, they make an incredible mess!

Figure 12

Size
- Will it fit the child?
- Will it fit in the child's home (figure 12)?

Value (for money and time)
- How much will the item cost?
- Could it be bought more cheaply somewhere else? (Check: other shops or catalogues; secondhand shops.)
- Would it be cheaper to make it? (Check: different materials; different suppliers.)
- How long will it take to make?
- Could it be made more quickly? (Check: different methods; different materials; different equipment.)
- How long will the child keep it? (Check: growth; changing tastes; old favourites – do you have any things that you have kept from your childhood?)
- Could it be passed on to another child? (Check: younger members of the family; friends.)
- Could it be sold when the child no longer needs (or wants) it? (Check: second-hand shops; small-ads.)

Examine carefully each item in your collection of children's textile items. Which places have had most wear? What might have caused that wear? Are there any ways the design or construction of the item might have been improved, so that it lasted longer? If you know the price, discuss whether it was good value for money.

See if you can persuade some parents to come into school and talk about the textiles that their children use.

It would be interesting to talk to children, too, and find out what they think about some of their clothes, toys or furnishings. If there are no young children near where you live, perhaps you could arrange to visit a local nursery, an infant or junior school, or a children's library.

Try to get to know one child really well: talk to the adults who look after him or her, as well as the child. Watch the child playing. Then make a checklist for designing or choosing a toy, a garment or a furnishing item that is exactly right for that child.

Look through mail-order catalogues, and visit some shops to see what is on sale. Compare the goods with your checklist – could you design something that would be better, or cheaper?

SEE ALSO

Choosing fabrics – for ideas about things to look for when choosing fabrics, or things made from fabrics.
Design – for help with designing things for children.
Properties of fibres chart – for help when you are deciding which fabric would be most suitable for a particular purpose.
Safety – for more about making things and places safer for children.

The book *Families and Child Development* (in this series) for more information about clothes, toys and safety.

Choosing fabrics

Collect some pictures of fabrics being used for different purposes; and samples of fabrics made from different fibres.

It is no good making all the right decisions about what you are going to make and how you are going to make it, if you choose the wrong fabric, as Jake and Mandy have in figure 13. Once the shop assistant has cut your cloth from the roll, you cannot change your mind and take it back. So it is worth thinking very carefully indeed before you spend valuable time and money on the fabric.

Properties of fabrics

Start by thinking about *who* will use the fabric, *how* it will be used, and *when* it will be used. What sort of job will it have to do? What *properties* must it have in order to do that job really well? The list below shows the sort of factors you will have to consider.

Will the fabric have to be:

- **Abrasion resistant** (stand up to a lot of rubbing without wearing out)?
- **Strong** enough to take a lot of strain without ripping (*tensile strength*)?
- **Washable?**
- **Boilable?**
- **Non-fade** (stand up to bright sunshine without the colours losing their brightness)?
- **Colour-fast** (be washed without any of its colour coming out)?
- **Non-shrink?**
- **Drip-dry** (dry quickly, and not need ironing)?
- **Windproof** (keep cold draughts out)?
- A good **thermal insulator** (keep the warmth of your body in)?
- A good **thermal conductor** (let the warmth of your body out)?
- **Absorbent** (soak up water, or sweat)?
- **Waterproof** (keep moisture out completely)?
- **Showerproof** (keep small amounts of moisture out for a while)?
- **Non-irritant** (comfortable against sensitive skins)?
- **Elastic** (stretch easily and then go back to its original size)?
- **Resilient** (go back, eventually, to its original shape when it has been crushed)?
- **Crease resistant** (stay crisp and smooth all day)?

Figure 13

- **Non-flammable** (not catch fire or burn easily)?
- **Thermoplastic** (soften when heated, so can be permanently pleated: may melt if pressed with a hot iron)?
- **Sunlight resistant** (stay in bright sunlight for a long time without getting weaker)?
- **Mothproof** (not attractive to the clothes moth)?
- **Rot-proof** (not damaged by damp, or sweat)?
- **Resistant to bleaches or chemicals?**

Figure 14 shows some examples of fabrics doing different jobs. What properties do you think are most important for each of them?
The first two have a "job description" (a *specification*) and a list of properties for you to put in order of importance. Add any properties you think have been left out, and then make your own lists for the last four examples.

Characteristics of fabrics

The way a fabric looks, feels, and behaves is important, too, if it is going to do its job well. So you should also think very carefully about its *characteristics*. Some of them will affect how the finished article looks, as well as how useful it is. Some of them will affect the techniques you use while you are working on the fabric. The list below shows the sort of characteristics you will have to consider.

- **Drape:** will the fabric be stiff enough or soft enough to create the shape you want?
- **Thickness:** will it be too bulky or too thin?
- **Weight:** will it be heavy enough or light enough to do its job well?
- **Texture:** will it feel and look right?
- **Transparency:** should it be *transparent* (see-through), or *opaque* (not see-through), or something in between (*transluscent*)?
- **Colour and pattern:** how important are these? Should the fabric look the same on both sides?
- **Loosely or tightly made:** will it matter if there are gaps between the threads, or if the threads are not firmly held in position?
- **Snagging:** are there any loose ("floating") threads or loops that might catch in things?
- **Width:** can you cut the shapes you need out of narrow fabric? Would a wide fabric mean more or less wastage?
- **Dimensional stability:** will it slither about and lose its shape, which could make cutting out difficult?
- **Fraying:** will this create problems when you are making it up? Will it make the seams weaker?
- **Hole-recovery:** will pinning or stitching make holes that will not disappear?

Motor bike "leathers"
Specification: allow easy movement but be close fitting to reduce "drag"; protect whole body in case of fire, being dragged along ground, or hitting sharp objects.
Properties:
mothproof; non-shrink; abrasion resistant; crease resistant; elastic; non-flammable; non-fade; good tensile strength.

Wedding dress
Specification: look attractive from front and back; suitable for travelling by car to and from ceremony, and kneeling for part of ceremony.
Properties: abrasion resistant; windproof; resilient; absorbent; rot-proof; crease resistant; non-irritant; non-flammable.

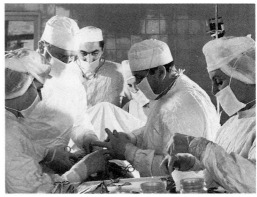

Operating gowns

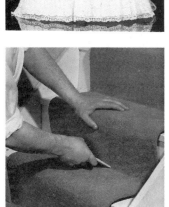

Stair carpet

Sails

Figure 14

Artificial turf

Figure 15 shows more pictures of fabrics doing different jobs. What characteristics do you think are most important for each of them?

As before, the first example has a specification and a list of characteristics for you to put in order of importance. Then work out your own specification and list of characteristics for the other examples.

Figure 15

Sportswear
Specification: allow complete freedom of movement even in strenuous activity; stand up to a lot of strain; comfortable.
Characteristics: close construction; opaque; elastic; thin; smooth.

Look at your collection of pictures of fabrics at work, write a specification for each of them and decide what properties and characteristics they would need. What properties do you think Jake and Mandy in figure 13 on page 19 should have been thinking about before they chose their fabrics?

Will a fabric do its job well?

You can find out quite a lot about a fabric just by examining it in the shop.

Look at the way it has been made. Is it a *twill*, or a *satin* weave? Is it a *pile* fabric? Is it *warp*, *weft*, or *raschel knit*? Is it *stitch-bonded*, or *laminated*? You need to know about most of the common ways in which fabric is made, because they give it so many of its properties and characteristics.

Look at the yarns it has been made from. Are they *staple* or *filament*? Are they *singles* or *ply*? Are they *hard* or *soft spun*? (See page 192.) If you understand what terms like these mean, the yarns can tell you a lot about how a fabric will look, feel, and perform.

While you are examining fabrics in the shop, you can also carry out some simple tests.

Is it crease-resistant? How resilient is it?
Crumple up a corner of each fabric and squeeze it gently for about a minute. When you let go, notice whether the fabric springs out with no creases, or just lies sadly crumpled in your hand. Give it a gentle shake; smooth the fabric out. How bad are the creases now?

How elastic is it?
Pull each fabric in different directions. How much does it stretch? Does it stretch the same amount in all directions? What happens when you stop pulling – does it go back to its original size and shape?

Will it be windproof?
Hold each fabric up to the light. How much light shows through it? Are the spaces between the threads big enough to let the wind through?

Will it resist abrasion?
Scrub each fabric against itself fairly hard. If the surface begins to fluff up fairly quickly, there is a chance that the fabric will not wear very well.

(If you notice some powder coming off the fabric when you scrub it, hold it up to the light. There may be quite wide spaces between the threads, where you have been rubbing. The powder is ''dressing'', it is used to fill up these spaces and make the fabric seem better quality than it really is. Once the dressing has worn off, the fabric will look very limp and threadbare. Do not buy it.)

How firmly is it made?
Squeeze the fabric between the fingers and thumbs of both hands: slide your thumbs away from each other. Do the threads slip apart?

Will it be comfortable?
Gently rub a corner of each fabric against your (clean) skin. Test it against the inside of your wrist, or on your neck – somewhere where your skin is particularly soft and sensitive.

Is it transparent?
Hold it up to the light and see how much it lets through. Put a patterned fabric behind it (black and white if possible) and see how clearly you can see it.

Will it fray?

Look at a raw edge, where the last piece was cut from the roll. Is there any sign of fraying? Rub it between your finger and thumb; pull gently, and see if the threads slide out easily.

Will it snag?

Look for long threads, or loops that might catch in things. If in doubt, gently scrape a corner (up and down, and from side to side) with your fingernail.

Is it the right thickness?

How stiff is it?

How heavy is it?

What are the colour and texture really like?

If you are buying a ready-made garment, you will discover these characteristics, (and some of the fabric's properties, too) when you try it on. If you are buying a length of fabric to make up yourself, you will need to unroll a couple of metres to find out about them. Unroll enough to let you arrange it over a display-stand, or hold it up against yourself. Look at it from a distance (in a mirror, if necessary). If fullness will be important, gather the fabric in your hands to see how it behaves.

You should always examine fabrics in this way before you make a decision about which to buy. Shopkeepers will not mind (because it will not cause any damage) and it will help you to make a wise choice. But they would mind very much if you tried to test a fabric to find out about abrasion resistance, tensile strength, flammability, absorption, or water-resistance.

The only way to find out, in the shop, about properties like these is to look at the label (figure 16). It will tell you things like the price, the width of the fabric (or the size of the garment) and the name of the manufacturer. But the most important piece of information it gives you is the name of the **fibre** the fabric has been made from. To people who understand them, these fibre names give important information about the fabric's properties.

When most people are choosing fabric, they start by deciding what they are going to make, and then look for the fabric with the right properties and characteristics for that particular purpose.

Some designers choose the fabric first (because they like the way it looks and feels), and then decide how they are going to use it. But they still have to know about its properties. If they did not, they would run the risk of making something that was quite unsuitable for its purpose.

Whichever way you work, the more fabrics you handle, the better you will become at choosing them. Here are some ways in which you can practise choosing fabrics.

Figure 16 A fabric label.

100% WOOL

192 cm wide

£8·50m

CJ 36B

479/21   3D

Use your collection of samples of different fabrics made from different fibres. Examine each one carefully (using a magnifying glass if you have one), and then write a very detailed description of it:

what it looks and feels like (remember to examine the front and the back);

how it was made;

the yarns and fibres it was made from;

and the properties and characteristics you would expect it to have.

You could then use these notes in two different ways:

1) Collect pictures of fabrics doing different jobs. Write a "job description" for each of them and decide which of your fabrics would do the job best.

2) Start with the fabric and design something (or several things) to be made from it, using its properties and characteristics to their best advantage.

Visit a fabric shop, taking with you a small amount of money and the fabric specification for something you have designed in school. Examine the fabrics on sale, and buy 0.10 m of the one that most nearly meets the specification.

Back in school, test the fabric for "invisible" properties like flame-resistance, absorption, tensile strength, abrasion resistance (see Tests on page 169). Then, with the help of your friends and your teacher, evaluate your choice of fabric.

Design and put up a display in your school, local library, or a local fabric shop that will help other people to choose fabrics wisely.

Ask your teacher to lend you a length of interesting fabric and a dressmaker's dummy. Collect pins, tapes, buttons and any other extras you think you may need, but no scissors. With a friend, pin the fabric to the dummy and create a garment by draping, gathering, pleating or folding the fabric.

If your teacher can supply you with several lengths of fabric, with very different characteristics, you could create a garment with each of them. Because you will not be cutting the fabrics, they can be unpinned and used again by other groups. (Try to photograph what you have done before it is unpinned.)

It would be interesting to see how much influence the fabric has on what you do, and what different groups of people do with the same fabric.

You can do something similar with shorter lengths of (uncut) fabric on a pin-board. Choose a subject like "Creatures" or "Strange Plants" or a well-known nursery rhyme, and create the shapes by pleating, folding, draping or bunching the fabric. You would need to work in a group to do this – one pair of hands is not enough to arrange the fabric, hold it in place, and pin it to the board.

You could do this in your classroom, but it might be more fun to work on the wall of a local nursery school, or in the children's section of the local library.

SEE ALSO

Fabric construction; Fibres; Fibres from animals; Fibres from plants; Knitted fabrics; Labels; Man-made fabrics; "Non-woven" fabrics; Properties of fibres; Woven fabrics; Yarns – for information about fibres, fabrics and yarns.
Labels; Rights and responsibilities for information about labelling and your rights as a consumer when choosing textiles.
Introduction; Design; and *Evaluation* for things to think about when choosing fabrics.

Textile Fabrics and their Selection, by Isabel B. Wingate (Prentice Hall Inc. NY).
The Fabric Catalog, by Martin Hardingham (Pocket Books New York – a Wallaby Book).
Textiles: Properties and Behaviour in Clothing Use, by Edward Miller (B T Batsford).
Textiles, by Norma Hollen, Jane Saddler, Anna L. Langford (Collier Macmillan Publishing, London).

KEY WORDS
Abrasion rubbing which can damage a material (or your skin).
Characteristics qualities that give a fabric its character – how it looks, feels and behaves.
Colour-fast does not fade or change colour because of washing or sunlight.
Dimensional stability how well a material keeps its shape.
Flame-resistant will burn, but not easily.
Flammable catches fire easily.
Hole recovery if needle or pin-holes disappear, a material has good hole-recovery (paper has poor hole-recovery).
Properties qualities that make a material suitable for certain jobs.
Specification a description of the job that a material or an article will have to do.
Thermal insulation keeping heat in.
Thermoplastic melts or softens when heated.

Colour

Collect catalogues, brochures and leaflets from firms like Laura Ashley, Dulux, Designers' Guild, Liberty, Dylon.
A variety of fabrics and yarns (including plastics).
Plenty of magazines and colour-supplements (dealing with fashion, general interest, home, food, photography, nature).
Some sheets of card (about 20 cm × 15 cm); glue (a rubber solution like Copydex is best when working with fabrics); a large, strong cardboard box; a craft knife; a strong lens, or low-power (×10 or ×20) microscope.

Before you read this section, find out what a *colour-wheel* is, and what the following words mean: *primary colours; secondary colours; contrasting colours; harmonious colours; tones; tints; shades.*

You will find some information about this in the book *Home and Consumer* in this series. Ask your Art teacher for help if you have any problems.

Colour is one of the most exciting parts of designing. It is often what you notice first about food, a room, a person's clothes, a bottle of shampoo, a car, or a piece of embroidery. It can make you feel calm or excited, happy or gloomy.

Every time you make a choice about textiles, colour is one of the first things you think about. How often do you bother to think about quality, price, shape and texture if you do not like the colour to start with?

Colour is a very personal matter – your likes and dislikes may depend on your age, your nationality, your family, and what suits your own colouring (or what you think suits you).

Things that have happened to you during your life can affect the way you feel about certain colours. For example, you may like or dislike a colour, or shade, because it reminds you of particular people or events.

This is why it is impossible to make a nice easy set of rules about colour that everyone can follow. What is right for you may be quite wrong for the people sitting next to you. It is also one of the reasons why, when new fabrics, yarns or fashions are created, they are usually made in several different *colourways*.

In picture 3 between pages 106 and 107 you can see a fabric printed in three different colourways.

Which is your favourite? Is it the same as your friends', or your teacher's? Is there one colourway that you, or they, really dislike? Discuss your feelings about these fabrics, and about your favourite colours with your friends. Can any of you work out why you feel the way you do about some colours, or certain shades of those colours?

Colour is said to be one of the ways in which we express ourselves. For example, we can show that we are one of the gang by choosing the same sort of colours (figure 17(a)), or we can show our independence by choosing something completely different (figure 17(b)).

Figure 17

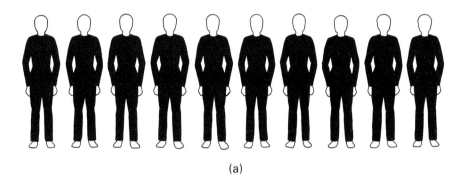

(a)

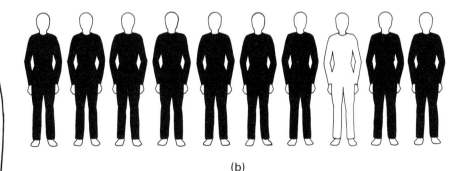

(b)

The colours people choose reveal a lot about their personalities. One quick glance at their clothes and their homes can tell you whether they are shy or outgoing, lively or quiet, respectable or rebellious.

Is this true? Find out by working with a small group of friends (make sure you are not sitting too close together).

Collect some pictures with colour-schemes that you like. Then collect sets of pictures that you think each of your friends would like. (Keep it private – do not let them see what you have chosen). When you have all done this, show each other the pictures you chose. Were you right about your friends' favourite colours? Were they right about yours?

Whether you guessed right or wrong, it would be interesting to discuss why you thought your friends would have chosen those colours. When you saw the colours they had chosen for themselves, was it a surprise to you? Did you learn something new about any of them? When they saw what you had chosen for them, were they surprised? Did they learn something new about themselves?

Managing colour

Some lucky people seem to have been born with a gift for colour. They seem to know, without being told, how to put colours together. The rest of us are not so lucky. We may know a beautiful colour-scheme when we see it, but we often find it very difficult to create one ourselves. This is why firms like Laura Ashley, Next and Colorol are so successful: they provide people with ready-made colour schemes. But you can learn how to manage colours yourself if you are prepared to work at it, and learn how to *look*.

Wherever you are, whatever you are doing, you will see colours. Sometimes you will see a mixture of colours that is so attractive it almost makes your mouth water. Sometimes you will see a colour-scheme that you simply hate. The next time this happens, stop for a moment and try to work out why you feel this way. Try to imagine what the colour-scheme would look like if you were to make one or two changes.

You will find some colour-schemes in picture 4, between pages 106 and 107. Do you like them? What do your friends think about them? Try to imagine what they would look like if one of the colours was changed. If you find it difficult to imagine what these changes would look like, try them out using paint, scraps of paper, or fabrics. Or you could use computer graphics, like Hex, Drawmouse, or Mosaic (details on page 37).

On the following pages are more ideas for ways in which you can find out about colour. Some of them would take quite a long time for one person to do. You may prefer to work in a group, with each person carrying out a different part of the investigation.

When professional designers are working with colour, they often get ideas from the world around them. Then they try out the ideas on a colour-board, mixing fabrics and yarns that match the colours they have seen. They like working with colour-boards because it is so quick and economical. You can see what one looks like in picture 5b, between pages 106 and 107.

The designer used the picture of the creature to help him create his colour-scheme. He first looked very carefully at the colours in the picture, and then tried to match them exactly with the yarns and fabrics.

Note The people who read this book will be using textiles in lots of different ways. To find out what the investigations mean in 'real life', try them out on some of the things you are designing as part of your course. The symbol  will remind you to do this.

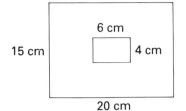

Figure 18 Home-made viewfinder.

Figure 19 There is a lot to see in a view like this. With a viewfinder you can look at just a small part of it, as the rectangles show. If you want to see more, move the viewfinder nearer your eye. If you want to see less, move it further away.

The colour-board in picture 5b is a piece of grey card, about 20 cm × 15 cm. The fabrics and yarns have been fixed in place with a very thin smear of glue (too much, and it would soak through and change the colours). Notice that there are no gaps between the fabrics and yarns: if the background card showed through, it would add another colour.

You can learn a lot about colour by copying the way designers work. Look at the colours in the world around you, and keep a record of what you see by making colour-boards. Take great care choosing the fabrics and yarns. Try to find exactly the same colours that you have been looking at. You may find a home-made viewfinder useful for this, because it helps you to focus on one small part of a scene.

To make a viewfinder, simply cut a neat hole in the middle of a piece of card. The viewfinder in figure 18 has a rectangular hole, but you might find it interesting to experiment with different shapes. You can also use your viewfinder in different ways (figure 19).

Look at the view from your classroom window, or take your viewfinder around the school grounds. Take it home and look at the view from your bedroom window, or a corner of your garden. Look at the same view at different times of the day, or of the year. Look at trees in autumn, a butterfly's wing, a sunset, a bunch of flowers, a

horse-race, a tennis match.

Look at some things more closely: the bark of different trees, an old wall or fence, a piece of fungus, the skin of an apple.

Use a hand-lens or low-powered microscope to look at colours really closely: the top of a carrot, a piece of moss or lichen, a piece of polished wood, a shiny beetle.

Think about proportion

Look again at picture 5, between pages 106 and 107, and you will see that the designer did not just copy the colours in the photograph. He also tried to use the colours in the same proportions (he tried to use same amounts of each colour). The main colours in the photograph are blue-black and white. There is quite a lot of coral, rust and beige, and a tiny flash of bright orange. The colour-board also uses lots of blue-black and white, less coral, rust and beige, and a few scraps of orange.

How important is proportion when working with colour?

Decide for yourself by making some colour-boards. Look through your collection of magazines, find a picture that you like, and make a colour-board, keeping as close as you can to the colours and proportions in the picture.

Then make two more colour-boards, using exactly the same colours and shapes as before. On the first colour-board, reverse the proportions of each colour used (where there was a large amount of a colour, use a small amount of it, and so on.) On the other one, use equal amounts of each colour.

Stand your colour-boards up and look at them from a distance. Has changing the proportions made any difference? Which of your colour-boards do you like best? Can you work out why? Ask your friends what they think.

Use crayons, or fabric collage, or torn paper shapes to find out how changing colour proportion would affect a piece of course-work you are planning.

Think about tone

It may sound odd, but black-and-white pictures can be very useful when you are working with colour. This is because they can help you to concentrate on the *tones* – the darkness and lightness of colours.

Tones can be just as important as colours, and the proportions in which the colours are used.

The same two colours can look very different together depending on whether they are the same or different tones.

A colour-scheme can look completely different if you change the tone of just one of the colours.

Tones can help you to create 3-D effects.

Do you think these statements are true? You can find out by collecting some coloured pictures; they will give you practice in seeing tones. Squint at them through half-closed eyes and try to decide which colours are the same tone. Use a photocopier to find out if you were right. Then use colour-boards to find out how you can make tones work for you.

darkest
lightest
darkest

Figure 20

lightest
darkest
lightest

Figure 21

Here are some ideas to start you off:

1) Collect fabrics and yarns that are the same colour, but different tones. This is called a *monochrome* colour-scheme (mono = one; chrome = colour).
   Arrange them in order, from dark to light.
   Then use them to make colour-boards like those in figures 20 and 21.
   Look at the colour-boards from a distance. Shut one eye and squint through the other. Do any of the boards have a 3-D effect?

2) Make another set of colour-boards, keeping the shapes and tones the same as before, but this time using more colours. (Check with the photocopier if you are not sure about some of the tones.) This is called a *multi-coloured* scheme (multi = many). Compare these with the monochrome colour-boards.

3) Can you have too many colours, or too many tones? Find out by making a series of colour-boards like this:
7 or 8 colours, all light tones,
7 or 8 colours, all dark tones,
7 or 8 colours, lots of tones of each colour.

3 or 4 colours, all light tones,
3 or 4 colours, all dark tones,
3 or 4 colours, lots of tones of each colour.

   Look at the boards from a little way away. Which one do you like best? Can you decide why? Do your friends agree? If you had used more colours, would it have made a difference?

Mixing colours

If you are working with dyes or inks, you can mix colours and make more colours. By adding black or white you can make your colours darker or lighter. But did you know that you can do the same thing with coloured fabrics or yarns?

Find out what happens when you make small samples, using two primary colours. Try different sized stripes or checks (you could knit, weave, stick or stitch them); figure 22 shows an example.

Figure 22

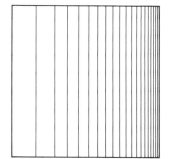 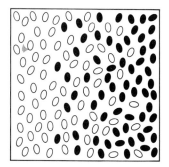

See what happens if you make dots all over a piece of grey fabric, starting with a different colour at each end and letting them mix together in the middle.

Pin your samples up and see what happens to the colours as you slowly walk away from them.

Think about texture

Because you are working with textiles rather than paint or paper, your colours will also have texture. Will these textures make any difference to your choice of colours? Try some of these ideas, and see what you think.

Make three colour-boards, using the same shapes each time:
1) one colour, lots of textures,
2) one texture, lots of colours,
3) lots of colours, lots of textures.

Cut a circle of fabric (about 15 cm diameter) into eight segments (figure 23(a)). Arrange the segments on a piece of card, all pointing in the same direction (figure 23(b)), and fix them in place. Try this with different fabrics: velvet, corduroy, satin, fur fabric, denim.

Figure 23
(*a*) *Fabric cut into segments.*
(*b*) *Fabric segments rearranged.*

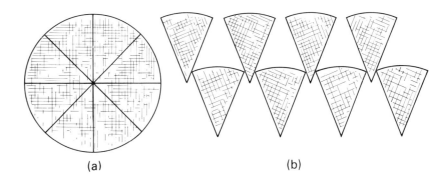

(a)   (b)

Work small experimental pieces of embroidery using the same thread all the time. Try blocks of straight stitches, going in different directions; or areas of different stitches creating different textures (figure 24). Make sure that none of the background fabric shows when the pieces are finished.

Figure 24

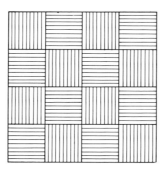 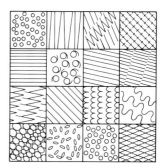

 Knitters or weavers could carry out a similar investigation, creating different areas of texture using the same yarn throughout.

You can find out more by noticing how the experts use texture. Whenever you see something made from textiles which attracts you, look at the textures as well as the colours. How many textures and colours have been used together? Would it look as attractive if there had been more or fewer textures?

Using a peep-show box

When you are choosing colours for a room, or deciding where to put a wall-hanging, you will probably need to consider where the light comes into the room.

A good way of investigating this is with a peep-show made out of a large cardboard box. Paint it white inside and then cut a window in one side, and a small hole to look through at one end (figure 25). Position the box so that as much daylight as possible is going in through the window hole.

Then stand one of your colour-boards (or a piece of knitting, embroidery or weaving) inside the box, put the lid on, and look at it

Figure 25 Peep-show box.

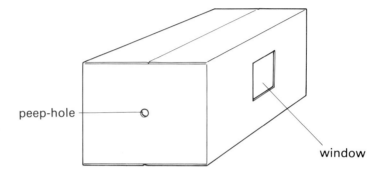

peep-hole

window

through the peep-hole. How does it look when it is:

opposite the window, with the light shining straight on it?

on the wall opposite the peep-hole, with the light coming from one side?

on the wall beside the window, with the light coming from behind?

Which position showed up the textures most?

You can use this peep-show box to try out different colour-schemes for rooms, as well. Start by putting "carpets" or "vinyl" on the floor (use pieces of cloth or paper); try different colours and different tones. With each floor-covering find out what happens if you change the colour of the walls. (You can do this quickly by pinning up sheets of plain paper.) Try the following:

a much lighter tone of the carpet colour,

a much darker tone of the carpet colour,

a contrasting or harmonising colour, in a darker or lighter tone, or in the same tone as the carpet.

Make "furniture" out of little boxes and wrap them in fabric scraps to find out what happens when you add more colours or tones to the room.

What does it look like if the carpet, walls and ceiling are all tones of the same colour, and you cover the "furniture" with a contrasting colour, or with a harmonising colour?

What happens if the furniture is the same tone and colour as the carpet, or as the walls? What if the furniture is a lighter or darker tone than the carpet?

How important is lighting?

The colours we use in our homes and for our clothes have to look good in daylight and in artificial light. You may already have noticed how difficult it is to match colours when you are shopping. What seems fine under the shop lights can look quite different when you get it outside. The weather can affect the way colours look, too.

You can find out more about colour and lighting by looking at some of your colour-boards and experimental samples under different types of light. The results may surprise you. Try some of these:
tungsten (an ordinary light-bulb),
fluorescent (remember these come in different colours),
ultra-violet,
candle-light,
sodium light (some street lights use this),
coloured bulbs or filters.

Do some colours or textures change more than others under certain lights?

SEE ALSO

Dyeing and printing for information about how textiles are coloured, and ideas for some investigations.

See the book *Home and Consumer* (in this series) for more about colour in the home.
If you want to find out more about the huge subject of colour, the following books will give you information and ideas.
Embroidery and Colour by Constance Howard (B T Batsford).
Arts and Design in Textiles by Michael Ward (Van Nostrand Reinhold).

The following computer programs enable you to experiment with colour.
Drawmouse, from Chelsea School of Art (address page 197).
Hex and *Mosaic*, from The Advisory Unit (was AUCBE) (address page 197).

Design

What does the word "design" mean? Look it up in some dictionaries and see what they say. You will probably find something like this:

Design – a plan, formed in the mind, of something this is to be made.

So "a design" means a lot more than "a drawing" or "a decoration". It is a plan showing how a particular problem can be solved.

The problem could be:

How can I make my garden easier to look after, and still have colour for most of the year? or

We need a new range of separates that will sell well in our High Street shops next winter; or

My friend wants a shelter for his horse; or

We want a large wall-hanging to decorate the entrance hall of our Head Office.

Design problems like these four cannot be solved without finding the answers to many questions.

Questions about *limitations*
- What job will the item have to do?
- What features must it have to do that job properly?

Questions about *needs*
- Who will use the item? When? Where?

Questions about *resources*
- How much time and money can be spent?
- What equipment and skills will be needed to make the item?
- What skills may be needed to use the item properly?
- How will the item be cared for?

In order to solve the problem, a good design must have these three features:

Appearance – will it look good?

Price – will it be worth the money?

Usefulness – will it do its job properly?

In this list, the features have been put in alphabetical order. Do you think it is also the right order of importance? Would it be the same for each of the problems above?

A successful design will also contain information about things like
- the materials to be used,
- how the item is to be made,
- colours, textures and decoration.

A painter can choose any imaginable shape. A designer cannot. If a designer is designing a bread knife, it must have a cutting edge and a handle: if he is designing a car it must have wheels and a floor. These are the sort of limitations which arise from the "function" of the thing being designed.*

* David Pye – *The Nature of Design*

Designers

People who get paid for designing things are called *professional designers*.

Some designers specialise in designing one thing: clothes; cars; shoes; houses (*architects*); printed, woven or knitted fabrics; gardens; rooms (*interior designers*), and so on.

Many large firms have designers on their payroll. Other firms call in a *freelance* or "product designer" when they need help with a particular product or project. These designers use their skills on a wide range of products. For example, Kenneth Grange designed a sewing machine for Frister and Rossman. He also designed a camera for Kodak, a razor for Wilkinson Sword and a food mixer for Kenwood.

Some magazines employ designers to help their readers with individual design problems, usually to do with things like colour-schemes, kitchens or garden plans.

Not many professional designers make the objects they have designed themselves; this is usually done by craftspeople in a workshop or factory. But they still have to know a lot about materials, equipment and how to make things. If they did not know about these they might design something that was impossible to make, or too costly, or that simply would not work.

How do designers work?

Most designers are concerned with creating something out of raw materials: metal, plastic, wood, yarns, fabric.

As you can see from figure 26, on pages 40 and 41, there is a lot of trial-and-error in Mark's work. However experienced they may be, designers can never be certain that their ideas will work. They have to try them out by making a 'model' (or *prototype*). Sometimes the model is of the whole item. Sometimes it is of one or two important parts of it.

Clothes are usually modelled in a cheap fabric called *mull*, but many textile items can be modelled in paper. For example, if you were designing a soft toy, you might make a paper model of it to check that it was the right size for the child, or to work out how the pieces should fit together. A design for embroidery or weaving might be tried out by sticking down shapes that had been cut or torn out of coloured paper.

Sometimes designers will have to experiment, to try out different colour-schemes, or find out the best way to do something. They will usually do this by making small samples in the same materials as they will use for the finished item.

Not all design problems are about making things. Figure 27 shows an example of a designer who solves problems by choosing things that have been designed by other people.

Figure 26

4 ONCE HE HAS CHOSEN THE SKETCHES THAT LOOK MOST PROMISING, MARK COMPARES THEM WITH HIS CHECKLIST OF WHAT THE BOSS WANTS

That collar would be difficult for a beginner to make...perhaps it would be better if I changed it to...

HE FINDS THAT HE HAS OVERLOOKED ONE OR TWO POINTS, SO HE MAKES A FEW CHANGES...

5 HE CAN'T BE SURE THAT HIS IDEAS WILL WORK UNTIL HE HAS TRIED THEM OUT IN 3D. SO MARK MAKES UP A SAMPLE OF EACH GARMENT IN A CHEAP FABRIC. AT THIS STAGE HE FINDS ONE OR TWO MORE THINGS THAT NEED CHANGING

That collar's much too big... the pleats don't work either...

perhaps it would be better to use gathers...

6 HAVING SORTED OUT THE MAIN PROBLEMS, MARK CAN DRAW HIS FINAL DESIGNS

...just staple the fabric samples on, and I can show them to the boss to see what she thinks of them...

7 ONCE THE BOSS HAS CHOSEN THE DESIGNS FOR THE CATALOGUE, MARK ASKS A MACHINIST TO MAKE THEM UP IN LOTS OF DIFFERENT FABRICS, TO FIND OUT WHICH ONES SUIT THE DESIGNS BEST

I'd like to try it in this corduroy, and a wool jersey, and that denim...

I'm not sure the style will work in the jersey, but I'll try it out just to make sure

Figure 26 continued

Figure 27 A window dresser at work.

Who else designs?

> We are all making choices and solving problems every day. So we are all designers.

Do you agree?

When you get dressed in the morning you are asking many of the same questions and making many of the same decisions as a professional designer. You, too, have to think about limitations, need and resources.

- Where am I going today?
- How long will I be wearing the clothes for?
- Do I need to keep dry, or cool, or warm?
- Will I get dirty?
- How do I need to look: sensible? attractive? fashionable? comfortable? clean?
- What sort of clothes will do the job best?
- What clothes can I choose from?
- Which shirt would be best?
- What else shall I wear with it?
- Does it need ironing?
- If so, have I got time to iron it, or should I choose something else?

a

b

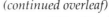

Picture 1   *See text on page 44.*
An example of a fashion student's work, showing some of the stages from design brief to finished garment.
a Initial rough sketches.
b One idea in more detail, including some photos that inspired it.
(continued overleaf)

c and *d* The finished dress.

c

d

Picture 2 *See text on page 44.*
More examples of fashion students' work.
Continued overleaf.

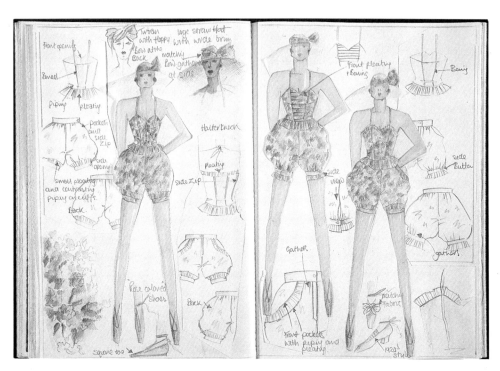

You may have to try on a few of your ideas first, before you can make a final decision. And at the end of the day you will *evaluate* what you chose.

— Did I feel comfortable?
— Did I look right?
— How well did the clothes do their job?
— If I could go back in time, would I change anything? Why?

What questions would you need to ask if you were tackling one of the design problems on page 38 or some of these below?

Your school is sending a team to a big international schools sports festival. They need a uniform and a set of banners to carry during the opening ceremony.

The children's library needs a new set of curtains, and covers for their floor-cushions.

You need a new rug for your hall floor.

A local shop wants a window display to advertise the latest sewing or knitting machine.

Would you need to make a model or prototype at any stage? Would you need to carry out any experiments? If so, when would this be? What would you be trying to find out?

SEE ALSO

The Introduction on pages 1 to 5.
Design sheets for help with recording your design work.
Exams, and *Evaluation*, for more about solving problems and making decisions.
Safety for some things to think about when you are designing.

Design Council Educational (address on page 198) for learning resource packs and the magazine *Designing* (published twice a year).

Design sheets

Some designers can do their thinking in their heads, but most of them find it easiest to think with a pencil in their hand, sketching out their ideas as they come to them. When they have chosen the most promising idea, they work on it in more detail. They will probably change it several times before they are ready to make a trial sample of it.

They make notes and sketches of all these changes as they work towards a final design. This helps them if they find that the idea they have chosen is not really going to solve the problem: they can go back through their notes and sketches to see whether one of their other ideas might be better.

They may find it helps to do careful drawings of some small details.

They then do a final drawing of their design, to show to their client or their boss.

Your design sheets will be useful to you in just the same way, but with one important difference. They are also a way of telling your examiner why whatever you have made looks the way it does.

As well as notes and sketches, your design sheets should include information about any research or experiments you have carried out, and all the samples you have made.

How you set out your design sheets will depend on several factors: your own likes and dislikes;
what you want to display;
how much there is;
the materials (paper, card, glue, and so on) that are available.

In picture 1 and picture 2, between pages 42 and 43, are a few examples that may give you some ideas.

SEE ALSO:

The Introduction on pages 1 to 5.
Design, and *Exams*, for more about explaining what you have been doing.
Research and investigation.

Techniques of Sketching, a Design Council Learning pack (address on page 198).

Dyeing and printing

Collect fabrics and yarns made from different fibres; some
household dyes; a medium-sized artist's brush; ink or food
colouring; a little plain flour; plain paper (plain newspaper is
ideal); old newspapers.

Figure 28
(a) Plain dyed fabric.
*(b) Woven check
fabric.*
*(c) Printed striped
fabric.*

Put a piece of cotton fabric (such as old sheeting) on a washable
surface. Dip a brush in ink or food colouring and paint your initials on
the cloth. Then thicken this "dye" with a little flour (it should be like
double cream) and use it to paint your initials on the fabric again.
Which initials are clearest?

When the fabric is dry, compare the feel of the two sets of initials.
Try to remove the dry paste, by scraping it off then rinsing it in warm
water.

This activity shows the basic difference between dyeing and printing. For dyeing, you need a liquid that will spread evenly through the fabric. It is difficult to create a pattern with liquid dyes because they run, so for printing the dye needs to be thickened, to stop it spreading out and blurring the edges of the pattern. Whatever has been used to thicken the dye needs to be removed.

The fabrics in figure 28 have had colour added in different ways. Dye was used for (a) and (b), and (c) was printed. As you can see, printing does not usually go right through the fabric. If you examine the coloured textiles around you, you can work out which were dyed and which were printed by looking at the back.

Fixing

Whether you are dyeing or printing, you have to make sure that the colour stays in the fabric. If your printed initials faded or disappeared when you tried to remove the paste it was for one of two reasons: either the colouring had not soaked right into the fibres; or it needed to be *fixed*, to make it stay there. Fixing is an extra process that nearly always has to be done after colour is added to textiles.

Dyeing

In their natural state, most fibres and filaments are off-white, cream or a shade of beige. So the very first textiles would have been rather pale, unless there were some black or brown sheep around.

Never happy to leave things as they are, human beings soon discovered how to liven up their fabrics with colour. They made most of their colours from plants, or from animals such as beetles (cochineal red) and shellfish (tyrian purple).

Until the middle of the last century, natural dyes were the only way of colouring textiles. Over the centuries, people became very expert at it. They were able to create wonderful, rich colours, using methods that were often extremely complicated and therefore very expensive.

You can make your own vegetable dyes by stewing skeins of yarn (pure wool is best) gently with some plant material. Try experimenting with things like onion-skins, blackberries, red cabbage, dock leaves. (See page 57 for a list of books about this fascinating craft.)

Everything changed in 1859 when the first synthetic dye was discovered, quite by accident, by a British chemist called William H Perkin. It made a very bright colour which he called mauve, and it caused a sensation (see page 75). Scientists were fascinated by this new chemistry of dyeing. They began to investigate why some dyes worked with some fibres and not with others, and began inventing ways to make more colours.

People soon found that synthetic dyes had several important advantages over natural dyes. Their colours were much brighter and clearer; they were much cheaper; they were easier to make; and because they were made to a scientific formula, colours could be matched exactly every time.

Synthetic dyes were so successful, and the new bright colours were so popular that by the beginning of this century they were used for most of the coloured textiles produced in Europe and America. Chemists are still developing dyes, and today dyers and printers can choose from thousands of different colours.

However, there are still two main problems to solve: the way different fibres take up the dye; and how permanent the dye is.

Different fibres

Try this investigation.

Collect scraps of white fabrics or yarns made from as many different man-made and natural fibres as you can find.

Label each fabric with the fibre content. Put them all in the same dyebath with any household dye; follow the dye manufacturer's instructions carefully. Rinse the fabrics thoroughly, and compare the results.

When they are dry, arrange your samples in order, from dark to pale. Which fibres have taken the dye best?

If you had used another type of dye, your results might have been quite different. Dyers and printers have to take great care choosing the right type of dye for each fibre they are working with.

Colour fastness

A truly colour fast dye will stay in the textile when it is washed, when it is exposed to sunlight, and when it is rubbed. It would resist damage by things like perspiration, bleaches and dry-cleaning fluids.

There is still no dye that can be guaranteed fast to everything. It may be fast to washing but not to sunlight. Or it might be fast to sunlight but not to perspiration.

So as well as choosing a dye that suits the fibre, dyers and printers must also think about what the textile is going to be used for. Although modern dyes are very efficient, it is always wise to test a fabric or yarn for colour fastness before using them.

Dyeing can be done at different stages during the manufacture of a textile, and it is given a different name according to that stage.

Spin dyeing

Colour can be added to man-made fibres while they are still liquid (see page 138). This is called *spin dyeing*.

Advantages
- Quick and easy – spinning and dyeing are done at the same time.
- Colours are very fast to light and washing.

Stock dyeing

Fibres can be dyed before they are spun into yarn. This is called *stock dyeing*.

Advantages
- The dye can get right into every fibre.
- Interesting yarns can be made, by mixing different coloured fibres.
- If two or more dyebaths do not come out exactly the same colour, the fibres can be mixed together to even out the differences.

Disadvantages
- It is not suitable for all fibres (cotton and flax are never stock dyed).
- By the time the fibres have been spun into yarn, woven or knitted, and then made up into garments or articles for sale, the colour may have gone out of fashion. This method is, therefore, only used for dyeing "safe" colours.

Yarn dyeing

Yarn can be dyed before it is made into cloth. This is called *yarn dyeing*.

Advantages
- It is cheaper than fibre dyeing.
- All types of fibres can be dyed at this stage.
- Interesting effects can be created by twisting different coloured yarns together.
- Patterned fabric can be made by weaving or knitting with two or more differently coloured yarns.

Disadvantages
- Because the fibres have been twisted together, the dye does not always soak into every fibre.
- There may be small differences in colour between one batch of yarn and the next. When the yarns are woven or knitted, these differences may show up as shadowy stripes.
- As with fibre dyed yarns, it is difficult to keep up with changing fashions.

Piece dyeing

Cloth can be dyed before it is cut and made up. This is called *piece dyeing*.

Advantages
- It is cheaper than yarn dyeing.
- Large amounts of undyed fabric can be made and stored, then small batches of the fabric can be dyed whatever colour happens to come into fashion.
- Interesting effects can be created if the fabric has been made from a blend or mixture of different (undyed) fibres. For example, if the warp yarns are acrylic and the weft yarns are wool, the fabric could come out of the dyebath with only the warp yarns coloured, or with warp and weft different colours.

Disadvantages
- The dye may not soak right through to colour all the fibres.
- If the fabric is rubbed, the lighter fibres inside the fabric may start to show.
- As with fibre and yarn dyeing, there may be small differences of colour from one batch to another.

Garment dyeing

Whole garments and articles can be dyed. This is *garment dyeing*.

Advantage
- Goods can be made up in large quantities, and then batches of them can be dyed in whatever colours are fashionable at the time.

Disadvantages
- If an article has been stitched together, the dye may not soak right through the stitching. If this happens, there will be light marks if anything needs to be unpicked.
- Details like top-stitching will also be dyed.

Printing

Printing happens after yarns have been made into fabric. There are three main types of printing in use today: *roller printing, screen printing* and *transfer printing*. As well as these, you may come across fabrics that have been resist printed, flock printed or duplex printed.

Most of these printing methods started as hand-crafts and then became mechanised. The fabrics you wear and use around your home will have been printed in factories, thousands of metres at a time.

The best way to understand these different methods of printing is to try them yourself. The instructions that follow are for a very simplified, experimental version of each method. There is no need to use fabric for these investigations – scrap paper or newspaper will do just as well. For your printing ink, you can use coloured flour paste (see page 45) or ready-mixed powder paint.

If you want to find out more, your school's Art Department may be able to help with equipment and advice. See also the book list on page 57.

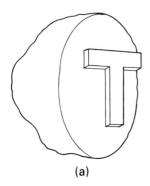

(a)

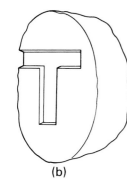

(b)

Figure 29 Potato printing.

Block printing and roller printing

This craft is over 2000 years old and, when done by experts using wooden or metal blocks, it can produce some exquisite patterns.
Start with this simple investigation.

You will need
two printing blocks, made from something that is flat and easy to cut into (a large potato cut in half, some lino, a block of balsa wood);
a sharp knife;
printing ink;
an old plate and a brush;
scrap paper, newspaper or scrap fabric for printing on.

1) Draw the same simple shape on each block.
2) Carve away the *background* from one of the blocks, so that the pattern sticks up in relief (figure 29(a)).
3) With the second block, carve away the *pattern*, so that it makes a groove in the block (figure 29(b)).
4) Brush a fairly thick layer of printing ink on the plate, dip your blocks in it and carefully press them on to the fabric or paper. (You may need to practise a little until you work out how much ink to use.)
5) Compare the results you get with each block. Which gives the best results?
6) Choose the block you like best, take a fresh sheet of paper, and print a neat, regular pattern all over it.
7) Time how long it takes.

Until 1785 all fabric printing was done by hand blocking – a very slow (and therefore expensive) method of decorating large quantities of fabric. Things speeded up a great deal when a Scotsman named Bell invented roller printing.

To find out what roller printing is like, you will need:
printing ink and a brush;
a large old plate;
some string (or scraps of thick cardboard) and glue;
a short roller (the inside of a toilet roll or a piece of thick dowel);
scrap paper or fabric to print on.

1) Cut the string or cardboard into small pieces and glue them all round the cylinder to make a pattern.

2) When all the pieces are firmly stuck and the glue is dry, paint a thick layer of printing ink on the plate.
3) Roll the roller in the ink until all the pieces of string or cardboard are coloured.
4) Carefully roll the roller over some scrap paper.
5) Time how long it takes to cover a sheet of paper the same size as the one you used for block printing.

You probably found that your roller ran out of ink by the time you got to the end of the paper. In factories, where machines do the printing, the rollers are inked automatically. You can see how this is done in figure 30.

Figure 30 Roller printing in a factory.

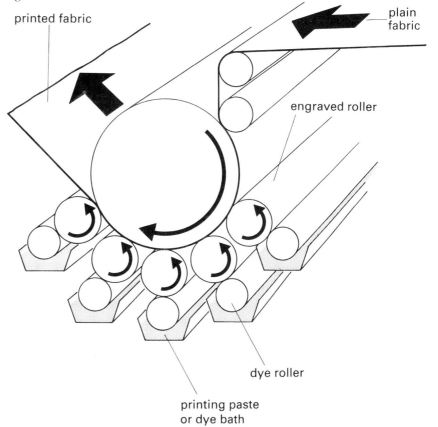

Some advantages of roller printing
● By using extra rollers one behind the other, fabric can be printed with several colours at the same time (some machines can print 16 colours at once).
● It is very fast – modern machines can print over 300 m of fabric per minute.
● It is cheap, once the rollers have been made and the machines set up.

Figure 31 Letters from stencil alphabet.

Some disadvantages of roller printing
● The rollers are very expensive to make.
Therefore, it is not economical to print less than 10 000 m of fabric with the same pattern.
● The size of the pattern is limited by the distance round the roller – pattern repeats cannot usually be much longer than 50 cm.
● It can be difficult to print large patches of colour without it looking blotchy.

Screen printing

This is a comparatively new method.

It developed from stencil printing, which was used a lot in ancient Japan. If you have ever used a lettering stencil you will understand one of the drawbacks of this method of printing. To stop the middle dropping out of some shapes, they have to be held in place with narrow strips (see figure 31).

When screen printing was invented, it meant that these strips were no longer needed. The stencil was stuck to a screen of fine silk fabric which held all the pieces in place; nothing could fall out.

For very simple screen printing, you will need:
a shallow cardboard box (e.g. the lid of a shoe-box);
a sharp knife;
some organdie or fine curtain net (the same size as the box);
masking tape or a stapler;
a strip of stiff card (about 10 cm deep and 1 cm narrower than the box);
printing ink;
scrap paper for printing on and for making the stencil (plain newspaper is ideal);
a pad of old newspapers.

1) Cut a rectangle out of the lid of your cardboard box (leave a margin of about 5 cm round each edge).
2) Use masking tape or staples to fix net over the hole. Stretch it as tight as you can, with no wrinkles. This will be your screen.
3) Take a piece of paper (as big as the box) and cut or rip some interesting holes in it. This is your stencil.
4) Put a piece of plain paper (which is your "fabric") on the newspaper pad, and lay the stencil on top of it (figure 32).
5) Put your screen on top of the stencil.
6) Pour a thick line of printing ink along one end of the screen.
7) Use the strip of card (your squeegee) to scrape the ink across the screen. Push down slightly when you do this – you are trying to press the ink through the screen. (See figure 33.)

Figure 32 Very simple screen printing.

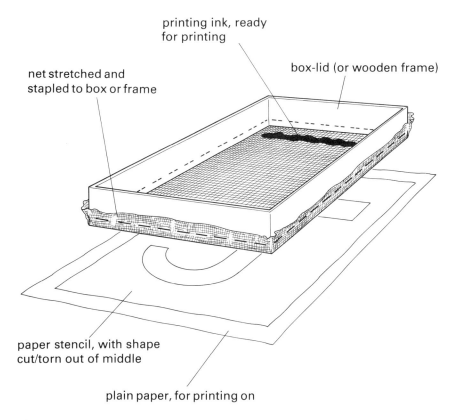

printing ink, ready for printing

box-lid (or wooden frame)

net stretched and stapled to box or frame

paper stencil, with shape cut/torn out of middle

plain paper, for printing on

8) Carefully lift the screen up. If all has gone well, you will find that your shapes are neatly printed on the paper and the stencil has stuck to the screen.

9) Compare your screen print with your block print. Which method do you think is best for printing large areas of colour?

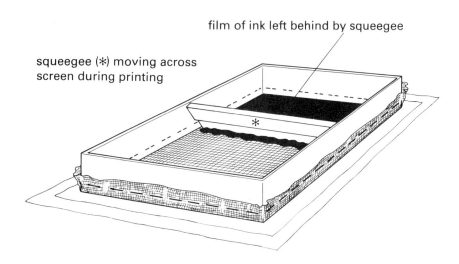

film of ink left behind by squeegee

squeegee (✳) moving across screen during printing

Figure 33 Use of the squeegee in simple screen printing.

If you want to make another print, next to your first one, you will either have to leave a gap or wait until the ink has dried. If you want to make a multi-coloured pattern, you will have to make more screens – one for each colour.

Until the 1950s screen printing was always done this way: the fabric was laid out on long tables (often more than 100 m long) and people moved along them, printing a small area at a time. It was a slow, difficult business, and screen printed fabrics were therefore very expensive. Now it is done by machine, which is very much quicker and cheaper.

Some advantages of screen printing
• Screens are fairly cheap to make, therefore it is economical to print smaller amounts of fabric.
• It is also easy to change to a new pattern.
• Very large patterns can be printed – they just need bigger screens.
• Large areas of colour or very fine detail can be printed equally well.
• Multi-coloured patterns can be machine-printed without much extra cost.

Some disadvantages of screen printing
• Hand printing is slow and needs very skilled workers.
• Machines are fast, but are very expensive to buy.

Transfer printing

This is a fairly new type of printing. It was not developed until the 1960s.

To explore transfer printing you will need:
Transfer Printing Inks (details on page 200);
some suitable fabrics (polyester usually works best, but you could also try nylon, acrylic, acetate and triacetate);
artists' brushes, and paper for painting on (plain newspaper will do);
an iron and ironing-board.

1) Use the inks just like water-colours, and paint a design on the plain newspaper. (Choosing colours can be difficult at first, because at this stage they all look very dull.)
2) When the ink is quite dry, put the paper face down on your fabric and go over it with a hot iron, moving the iron slowly and steadily.
3) Lift up a corner of the paper and look at the fabric – the colour should have been transferred to it.
4) If the colours look rather pale, replace the paper and go over it again with the iron.

Some advantages of transfer printing
● Fabrics, or complete garments, can be printed with a multi-coloured design in one step.
● Colours can be pale and delicate, or very brilliant.
● The colours are permanent – there is no need for a separate fixing process.
● The equipment for industrial transfer printing is fairly simple.
● Printers can buy ready-printed paper, or have special designs made for them. They do not have to spend time and money preparing screens or engraved rollers.
● If something goes wrong it is nearly always when the design is put on the paper. Therefore mistakes are not so expensive as with other printing methods, where mistakes can mean that a whole roll of fabric is ruined.

Some disadvantages of transfer printing
● The high temperatures that have to be used can damage some fabrics.
● It is difficult to judge what the colours will look like until they have been transferred to fabric.
● The process does not work as well with natural fibres (although scientists are working on this.)

Some less common printing methods

Flock printing

1) Decorate some fabric with dots or lines of glue and then scatter glitter all over it.
2) Shake the cloth over some newspaper to get rid of the spare glitter.

You may have seen fabrics and wallpapers decorated in this way – not with glitter, of course, but with tiny fibres.

Duplex printing

1) Print a pattern (something simple, like large dots) on fabric or paper.
2) When it is dry, turn it over and print the same pattern on the other side.

If a reversible fabric is needed (for curtains, perhaps) it is sometimes printed on both sides. In factories this is done either by putting the fabric through the machine twice, or by using a special duplex machine which prints both sides at once.

Discharge printing

Put tiny dots of bleach on a dyed fabric (take care not to splash it on your clothes) and see what happens.

When you see a dark fabric with a pattern of white or light coloured dots, this is one of the ways it could have been done. Printers do not just drop bleach on the fabric, of course. They use special chemicals that will remove the dye without damaging the fabric, and they make the chemicals into a paste so that they can print sharp, clear shapes.

Resist printing

1) Light a candle and let the wax drip on to a piece of cloth.
2) Dye the cloth (or simply brush some ink or food colouring over it).
3) When it is dry, scrape the wax off.

This is another way of creating light patterns on a dark background – by preventing the dye from reaching certain parts of the fabric. In industry the pattern is printed on the cloth using a special paste (not wax) that will resist the dye.

When you dripped candle-wax on your fabric you were doing a simple type of *batik*, a very ancient method of decorating fabric.

Another resist technique is tie-dye.

Imagine that you were going to make one or more of the following for part of your course-work, and you wanted to add colour to it in some way: a knitted sweater; a wall-hanging; a curtain; an embroidered chess-set and board; a quilted bed-cover or cushion; a summer shirt.

Which method (or methods) would you use to add the colour, and when would you do it?

SEE ALSO

Colour for help with exploring colour.
Man-made fibres for information about how man-made fibres are made.
Properties of fibres for information about the absorbency of different fibres.
Yarns for information about how yarns are made.

Beginner's Guide to Fabric Dyeing and Printing by Stuart and Patricia Robinson, published by Newnes Technical Books.
The Weaving, Spinning and Dyeing Book by Rachel Brown, published by Routledge and Kegan Paul.
Dyes from Natural Sources by Anne Dyer, published by G Bell & Sons.
Spinning and Dyeing the Natural Way by Ruth A Castino, published by Evans Bros.
Dyes from Plants by Seonaid Robertson, published by Van Nostrand Reinhold.
Ideas and Techniques for Fabric Design by Lynda Flower, published by Longman.
A History of Dyed Textiles, by Stuart Robinson (Studio Vista).
Woad in the Fens, by Norman T. Wills (L J Ruskin & Sons, Sibseyu Lane, Boston, Lincs.).
The Thames and Hudson Manual of Dyes and Fabrics, by Joyce Storey (Thames and Hudson).
The Thames and Hudson Manual of Textile Printing, by Joyce Storey (Thames and Hudson).

KEY WORDS

Fixing Making sure that the colour is firmly fixed to the fibre, yarn or fabric. Sometimes done by treating the fibres before they are dyed, or by mixing a chemical with the dye itself, or after dyeing.
Synthetic artificial; not natural.

Equipment

Collect adverts, leaflets, catalogues and price lists for textile equipment.

Take one craft which is taught in your school, and make a list of all the equipment that is provided for it. If you can, find out what each item would cost to buy.

Most textile crafts need some equipment. It may be something very simple, like a pair of knitting needles. It may be very complicated, like a knitting or sewing machine.

During your textile course you may have had a chance to use different versions of each type of equipment. If so, you will already know that some makes or models are much more popular than others. There is often a queue to use some of them, while others sit on the shelf completely unused.

Discuss: Which are the most popular pieces of equipment in your textiles room? Which are the least popular? Why?

Has your experience in school put you off buying any particular makes or models of equipment? (When you are thinking about this, remember that equipment gets more use in one year at school than it would in ten years in most people's homes.)

Choosing equipment

If you want to carry on with your textile craft when you leave school, you will want some equipment of your own.

What will you need? The answer to this question will depend on:
- which craft or crafts you are interested in; (some pieces of equipment, like scissors, are needed for most textile crafts, others, like looms or sewing machines, are more specialised).
- how important your craft will be in your life – your main hobby, a way of earning money, or just a useful skill?

Look at your list of school equipment, and give each item a star rating, according to how important you think it is.

You might give three stars to the really basic essentials, which you could not possibly do without. For most crafts these will be the same simple pieces of equipment that have been used for hundreds of years.

You could give two stars to the things that you would find really useful, either because they would save you time, or because some processes would be impossible without them.

One star could apply to items you would love to own, but will probably have to manage without for the time being, until you have saved up.

Once you have decided what items of equipment you need, your next problem will be choosing which brand, and which model. To help you do this, you will need to ask yourself a lot of questions.

Questions about your needs
- Will you need to carry it around, or move it from place to place?
- How hard-wearing will the equipment need to be?
- How much will you use it: every day, a few times a week, a few times a month?
- What will you use it for: light, delicate work, heavy work?
- Will you use it for one special type of work, or for lots of different types?

Questions about your resources
- How much can you afford to spend?
- Where will you keep it? (Size might be important.)
- How expert are you? (Will you be able to make full use of an advanced model with lots of special features? If not, will you become more expert in time? Or would something simple suit you better?)
- Will it be easy to buy spares, extra accessories, or to get it repaired? How much will these cost?

The answers to these questions will make a useful checklist when you begin to investigate what is available. You would not need to ask all these questions about every single item of equipment: go through your list and decide which questions are important for each item.

Value for money

You can find out what is available by visiting shops and exhibitions, collecting leaflets, and reading magazines. Once you have compared what is available against your checklist, you will probably find that you are left with a choice between three or four different makes or models.

To help you decide, look for reports in recent copies of *Which?*, *Good Housekeeping* or some of the specialist magazines. If you can only find fairly old reports, they are still worth reading because they can give you ideas about what to look for when you are comparing pieces of equipment.

Visit shops, and ask for the equipment to be demonstrated. Take along some of your own material, and ask if you can try using the equipment yourself. Many shops will give lessons on using equipment that has been bought there. If your local shop does not do this, find out whether there are any evening classes that might help you.

Top quality make. Basic model. Second-hand. £80.

Ordinary make. Latest electronic model. New. £80.

Figure 34

New or secondhand?

Figure 34 shows a choice you may be faced with when you are buying equipment. Discuss with some friends which you would buy if you saw these labels on various pieces of equipment, and why.

What do you think are the advantages and disadvantages of buying new and second-hand?

Is there any equipment that you would never buy second-hand?

Look at the people in Figure 35, and read the following descriptions of them. Can you find the equipment that would suit each of them?

Figure 35(a) shows Mrs Ahmed, who saves money by making some of her family's clothes. She has just made her first set of curtains and is very pleased with the results. At the moment she has to work in the dining-room, which means that everything has to be cleared away for meal-times. Her present sewing-machine is a very heavy hand-operated model.

Her parents have promised to buy her an electric machine that will do a zig-zag stitch, but cannot afford to spend more than £150.

Figure 35
(*a*) Mrs Ahmed and children
(*b*) Angie
(*c*) Mr Nichols
(*d*) Julie and Adam

Angie, in Figure 35(b), started hand-knitting two years ago, when she found it was the only way to get the sweaters she wanted at a price she could afford. She soon became fascinated by texture, and spent a lot of time experimenting with different yarns and stitches. She has just finished her first year at Art College, and is getting very interested in machine-knitting. She likes its speed, and the way it allows her to use very fine yarns as well as thicker ones.

She would like to have her own machine, and can afford up to £200 but is prepared to buy on hire purchase, if the repayments are not too high.

Figure 35(c) shows Mr Nichols who will soon retire, and is looking forward to spending more time on his hobby – spinning and weaving. He likes working on a large scale, and has completed several rugs and wall-hangings. He likes using a wide variety of yarns, and often finds it difficult to buy exactly what he wants. He sometimes spins his own yarn using a drop-spindle, but finds this rather slow.

His colleagues at the office are collecting to buy him a leaving present. They have told him they expect to have quite a large sum, so he has asked them to buy him a spinning wheel with which he can create really unusual yarns.

Julie and Adam, Figure 35(d), have just moved into a small flat. Like most young couples, they have very little money to spare. They have bought some cheap second-hand furniture which they are doing up. There are shabby old curtains on the windows, but Julie and Adam have got to make do with them until they have something to put in their place. Because it would be so expensive to buy all the furnishing fabric they need (as well as new curtains they have got to cover a sofa and several chairs), they want to print their own. They were both good at art when they were at school, and Julie became very keen on textile design, expecially screen-printing.

They need enough equipment to enable them to print quite long lengths of fabric but it must be cheap.

To choose the pieces of equipment you think would be best for these people, use your collection of leaflets. Look at advertisements in newspapers and magazines. Visit shops, and follow up the small-ads in your local newspaper and in the newsagent's window.

Caring for equipment

However careful you are about choosing equipment, you cannot expect it to go on working properly if it is misused.

The best scissors in the world will soon lose their cutting edge if they are used on paper or for cutting through too many layers of tough denim. A machine with moving parts will seize up if it is not regularly oiled in the right places. Wooden or metal parts will bend or break if they are strained or knocked.

With a group of friends, choose an item of equipment and find out how it should be used and cared for to keep it in good working order.

You can get this information from: instruction books or leaflets that come with new equipment; specialist books or magazines; shopkeepers; experts (craftspeople, teachers, members of craft groups or clubs).

Share your knowledge with the rest of the group. You could: write instructions; draw diagrams; make a list of do's and don'ts; put up a display (a shopkeeper or craftsperson may be able to lend you some examples of equipment that has been damaged because of carelessness or ignorance); give a demonstration (and video-tape it, for your teacher to use with younger classes).

Repairs and servicing

Just like a car or motor-bike, most textile equipment needs regular servicing by an expert to keep it in perfect working order. Blades need to be sharpened; nuts and bolts need to be tightened; some moving parts may need adjusting; others may wear out and have to be replaced.

Find out what would be the annual running costs of the equipment you listed at the start of this Topic. Include things like scissor-sharpening. (Do you know where you can have this done?) Your local suppliers will tell you how much a standard service costs, and how often it needs to be done. Ask them what the most common repairs are, and how much they cost.

SEE ALSO

Advertising for help with understanding how manufacturers and retailers try to persuade you to buy their products.
Instructions for help with using the instructions that come with new items of equipment.
Rights and responsibilities for information about your rights and responsibilities when buying equipment.
Safety for things to think about when buying and using equipment.
Shops for information about the choices of where to buy and how to pay for items.

Evaluation

Evaluating is something we all do when we have designed, made, or bought something.

Whenever you say to yourself

That was a real success, because...

It was a complete waste of time and money because...

If only I could go back to the beginning and do it all over again...

you are making an *evaluation*

Each time you make an evaluation, however simple, you are storing up knowledge for future use. Some people call it "learning by experience". There is an example of a very simple evaluation in Figure 36.

Figure 36 "Look at what I've made – isn't it great?

"You can open it here, so the pilot can eject if there's an emergency.

"The wings would look better if they were all blue, but I didn't have enough blue bits. You've got to be careful that the back end doesn't drop off when you pick it up. I think it would have been stronger if I'd used longer pieces there. . . ."

The little girl in Figure 36 has thought about
the appearance of her model;
its function (what it will do, how well it does it);
its quality;
how long it took (and whether it was worth the effort);
how she could have made it better (she will remember that when she makes her next model).

Like most young children, she did not start with a clear idea of what her model was going to be. You may be able to remember being like this when you were a child. Now, when you are designing (or making, or buying) something, you do it with certain needs in mind, and you will have worked out a clear idea of what you want to end up with.

As you work towards solving your problem you will find that you are carrying out several 'mini-evaluations'. For example,
- when you look at your first sheet of rough sketches and decide which is the best idea;
- when you try out several different techniques, to find out which one is best for a particular yarn or fabric;
- when you investigate different materials, to find out which will do a particular job best;
- when you make a model or prototype to find out how well your idea will work.

See also picture 1, between pages 42 and 43, for another illustration of this.

When you make your final evaluation, you will be looking at several things:
- What was the original problem?
- Have you solved it?
- How well have you solved it?
- What are you particularly pleased with about your result?
- What do you think could have been better?
- How could this have been done? (If you could start all over again, what would you have done differently?)

If evaluation is an important part of your exam, try to practise doing it as often as you can. Start with something simple: getting ready for school in the morning; doing your homework; catching the bus; boiling an egg; washing your socks. As you get used to it, try evaluating more complicated problems: cooking a meal; repainting your bedroom walls; planning a party; buying new shoes.

Practise writing things down: the problem; how you tried to solve it; your evaluation.

If your problem was an every-day one, like getting ready for school, you can use your evaluation to help you solve it better tomorrow, and then evaluate *that* activity.

SEE ALSO

Design, Design sheets, Exams, for examples of situations when you will need to carry out an evaluation.
Equipment, Shopping, to help you evaluate things you will buy.

KEY WORDS
Prototype a trial version of an item (or part of an item).

Exams

Figure 37

Figure 38

Is Figure 37 how you see exams? If so, try not to because they are not meant to be like that at all. From the examiners' point of view, exams look more like Figure 38.

Examiners are not trying to find out what you do not know, and what you cannot do – they are trying very hard to find out what you *do* know, what you *can* do, and how you will use this knowledge and skill in real life.

Your teacher has a booklet that explains what the examiners are looking for. It is called a syllabus. One part of the syllabus tells your teacher what knowledge the examiners would like you to have. Another part describes the *abilities* they want you to show, which could be as listed below.

a) Can you *analyse* a problem and work out:
the needs of the people involved;
the most important things you should take into account when you are solving the problem.
(see *Introduction; Children; Design*)

b) Can you work out what *knowledge* you will need to solve the problem?
Can you remember, or find this knowledge? (see *Research*)
If information is in the form of a graph, chart or table, can you get the facts you want from it?
Can you follow instructions? (see *Instructions*)
Can you find out other facts by carrying out tests or investigations? (see *Research and investigations; Tests*)
Can you use this knowledge in a sensible way?

c) Can you *plan* what you are going to do so that you get the best result?

d) Can you carry out your plan, using the most suitable skills and equipment?
(see *Equipment; Mistakes; Safety; Shopping*)

e) Can you *evaluate* what you have done?
(see *Evaluation*)

To give you a chance to show all these different kinds of abilities, your exam will be in different parts: written papers, and a practical and coursework assessment.

Written exams

Each question will have been designed with great care to find out about some of your abilities. So when you are doing a written exam, read the questions very carefully. Try to work out what the examiner wants to find out about you.

Once you have done that, make it as easy as possible for the examiner to mark your work:
• Make sure your writing is easy to read.

- Keep your answers as brief as possible.
- If the question is complicated, give each point a number, and start each on a new line.
- If what you want to say is difficult to describe, a clearly labelled diagram may solve your problem.

If you can, get hold of some specimen exam questions and practise answering them with your friends. Start by discussing each question, trying to decide exactly what the examiner wants to find out. Then practise writing the answers. You could do this in several ways:

- work in pairs, discussing what the answer should be, and the best way of writing it down;
- work on your own, mark your partner's answers, and then discuss what you have done with the rest of the group;
- once you have decided what the answer should be, try writing it down in different ways (numbered paragraphs or sentences; a list; diagrams).

Notice how long each type of answer takes. Ask your friends to help you decide which type of answer is clearest.

Practical exams and coursework

Solving problems in a practical way is such an important part of Home Economics, it is natural that it should be an important part of the exam as well.

This part of the exam is designed to test all the abilities listed on page 66, so it gives you a wonderful chance to show the examiners what you can do.

Each examining board has its own way of organising this part of the exam (your teacher will be able to give you exact details of what your examining board wants) but most of them ask you to make something. This is so that they can find out about your practical skills, and how well you manage your resources.

If you have a choice about what you make, or how you make it, take great care to choose wisely. Remember, you are trying to show the examiners what you *can* do, not what you cannot do. For example:

- If you are an expert on the sewing machine, could you show this off by adding lots of top-stitching, or free embroidery in your design?
- If you cannot handle a particular fabric or yarn really well, or if you cannot make a particular fastening well, would it be sensible to choose a different fabric, yarn or fastening?

Decisions like these will give the examiners a clue about how well you manage your most important resource – yourself.

They will also be interested in how you manage other resources like time, money and equipment. For example:

- If you only had a few weeks, would it be wise to design a full-length hand-knitted coat in a fine yarn?
- If you only had a few pounds to spend, would a pure silk bedspread be the best choice for a batik?

The stages you go through before you actually begin making an item, or while you are carrying out an investigation, are very important, too. Your teacher will be able to tell you just how important your examining board thinks they are. (Some examiners think they are more important than the item itself.)

In an ideal world you would have your own personal examiner who would watch you go through all these stages. He or she would be able to see at first-hand exactly how much thought, research, investigation and planning had gone into making your finished item. But it is not an ideal world, so the examiners have to rely on you to tell them what you did, and why you did it. This is why most of them ask for a record of what led up to your finished item, and that is why it is so important to give a really clear account of what you have done.

Do not rely on memory for this: write down or sketch all your thoughts, and keep absolutely everything, however rough it is. You can always tidy everything up at the end, when you have decided what to include in your final record of work.

Gathering all this material together, sorting it out, and getting it ready for the examiner may take longer than you think, so do not leave it until the last minute. When you start a practical course, the end always seems a long way off. But as the exam draws nearer, time begins to play tricks on you – the last few weeks can seem to flash by at an amazing speed. Show the examiners that you can manage time efficiently by planning your work carefully, and making sure that you do not have a last-minute panic.

You will find more information about records of work on page 44.

SEE ALSO

Introduction, Design, Equipment, Instructions, Tests, for more ideas and information.

The book *Families and Child Development* (in this series) (XYZ) for advice about preparing for exams.

KEY WORD
Syllabus a booklet that describes the knowledge and skills the examiners will be looking for, and how they will try to find it out.

Fabric construction

Collect fabric scraps (as many as possible); a magnifying glass or yarn counter (×20); a low-power microscope (×40).

Examine your collection of fabric scraps carefully using a lens, and looking at both sides of each fabric. Then sort them into sets. You will probably find that most of them fall into one of these three groups.

a) **Fabrics made from yarns – woven** (figure 39)
How to recognise woven fabrics
1) You will see two sets of threads – one going up and down the fabric, the other going from side to side. The threads are interlaced (they pass over and under each other).
2) The cut edges will fray.
3) The fabric will stretch more if you pull it diagonally (×) than if you pull it along the threads (+).
   There are three basic weaves. From these we get hundreds of different woven fabrics.
   You can find out more about woven fabrics on page 181.

Figure 39 A selection of woven fabrics.

b) **Fabrics made from yarns – knitted** (figure 40)

*Figure 40 A selection
of knitted fabrics.*

Figure 40 A selection of knitted fabrics.

How to recognise knitted fabrics
1) The thread (or threads) will be looped round each other.
2) Cut edges will not fray (but a broken thread may cause a ladder).
3) When pulled, they may stretch vertically (I), horizontally (−), or diagonally (×).
4) Some knitted fabrics will curl up at the edges.
   There are two basic types of knitting, from which we get dozens of different types of knitted fabrics.
   You can find out more about knitted fabrics on page 122.

c) **Fabrics made from fibres ("non-woven" fabrics)** (figure 41)

*Figure 41 A selection
of "non-woven"
fabrics.*

Figure 41 A selection of "non-woven" fabrics.

How to recognise "non-woven" fabrics
1) There are usually no threads to be seen.

2) Fibres usually run in all directions.
3) Cut edges do not fray.
4) When pulled (in any direction) the fabric will usually stretch very little.

   There are two basic ways of making fabrics direct from fibres.

   You can find out more about these ''non-woven'' fabrics on page 145. You may also find . . .

d) **Laces and nets** (figure 42)

Figure 42 Laces and nets.

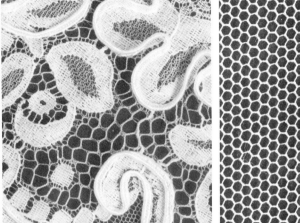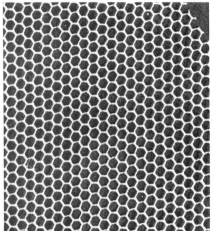

How to recognise lace and net fabrics
1) They are made from very fine threads, which are twisted together.
2) The structure is very 'open' – designs are made up of a series of holes.
3) Unless they have been specially stiffened, laces and nets are easily pulled out of shape.

e) **Fabrics made from sheet or film** (figure 43)

Figure 43 A selection of sheet or film fabrics.

How to recognise fabrics made from sheet or film
1) There are no threads *or fibres* to be seen.
2) Cut edges do not fray.
3) When pulled (in any direction) there is very little stretch.

f) **Combination fabrics** (figure 44)

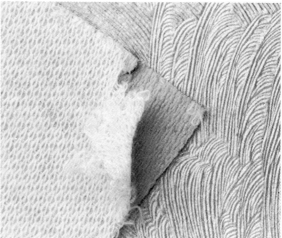

Figure 44 A selection of combination fabrics.

How to recognise combination fabrics
1) Two or more layers can be peeled apart.
2) Front and back of the fabric may show different types of construction (knitted + film; woven + knitted).

Why are there so many ways of making fabrics? One answer could be "Because we need to use fabrics in so many different ways". But you could also say "We use fabrics in so many ways because there are so many different ones available". What do you think? Here are some possible reasons for you to discuss.

For aesthetic reasons (Aesthetic means "the appreciation of beauty") Appearance is usually (though not always) very important for things made from textiles. The way a fabric is made can change how it looks, feels and behaves.

For practical reasons
The way a fabric is made can give it qualities (like elasticity, transparency, toughness) that make it suitable for different jobs. It can also affect how easy or difficult the fabric is to cut and sew.

For economic reasons
Cost is often a very important factor in choosing fabrics. Some ways of making fabrics are much quicker (and therefore much cheaper) than others. Another way to keep costs down is by using fabrics that are easy (and therefore quick) to cut and sew.

For technical reasons
Many different ways of making fabrics have become possible because of new technology and new fibres. These new fabrics have qualities (aesthetic, practical or economic) that are different from those of fabrics made in traditional ways.

Find out what these different types of fabric are used for by going on a Fabric Hunt. (Take a magnifying glass with you.)

Start by looking at the fabrics you and your friends are wearing, and at the fabrics used around your school. (Ask the caretaker if you can look at overalls, dishcloths and dusters.) Examine fabrics in your home and in the shops – clothes, furnishings, towels, tea-towels, car seats, goal nets. Make a list of all the things you find that are made from woven, knitted, lace or net, "non-woven", sheet or film, and combination fabrics.

Which type of fabric seems to be used most?

Are there some things that nearly always seem to be made from the same type of fabric? (If so, what are they, and why do you think this is?)

SEE ALSO

Knitted fabrics
"Non-woven" fabrics ⎫ for information about how these different
Woven fabrics ⎭ fabrics are made.

Textiles: Properties and behaviour in clothing use, by Edward Miller
(B T Batsford Ltd).
Textile and Weaving Structures, by Peter Collingwod (B T Batsford
Ltd) for information about unusual ways of making fabrics.
Handbook of Textiles, by A M Collier (Wheaton).
The Fabric Catalog, by Martin Hardingham (Pocket Books New York).
Textiles, by N Hollen, J Saddler and A L Langford (Collier
Macmillan Ltd).
Lace, by L W van der Muelen-Nulle (Merlin Press).

KEY WORD
"Non-woven" fabrics this name has been put in quotes because it is
not a true description of the fabrics. There are many fabrics that have
not been woven (lace, net and knits for example), but they have been
made from yarns, and are not described as non-woven fabrics. In the
textile industry, the term "non-woven" is used to describe fabrics that
have not been made from yarns.

Fashion

Collect new and old copies of *Vogue, W* and other fashion magazines; catalogues; newspaper articles about fashion; photos of different figure types (e.g. "before" and "after" photos from dieting adverts).
(Find numbers going back as far as possible; your local library may have some in its reference section.)
If you are lucky enough to have an art college with a fashion department near you, ask if you can look through their collection of fashion magazines and books.

Fashion is such a huge, mysterious subject that it would need a book twice as big as this one to explore it.

Luckily there is no shortage of books and articles about fashion. Some of them are useful if you want facts about what people wore in the past. Others are interesting if you want to work out why people wore those clothes. You will find a list of some of these books at the end of this Topic. Before you begin reading them, do some thinking of your own about fashion as it is now.

Do you agree? Imagine what it would be like if today's fashion went on, without changing, for a hundred years. Could it still be called a fashion?

> If there was no change, there would be no fashion - just clothes.

Why do fashions change?

There is no one answer to this question. Here are some ideas for you to think about.

Inventions

This happened when aniline dyes were discovered in 1856: suddenly 'mauve' became the most fashionable colour to wear.

> The discovery or invention of new fabrics or techniques can create new fashions.

When stretch yarns (elastomeric fibres and Helanca) were developed in the 1950s, everybody wanted to wear ski-pants (figure 45). And the new stiffened nylon (known as 'paper nylon') created a fashion for skirts that were almost as wide as crinolines.

Some people say that the fashion for shorter and shorter skirts led to the development of tights: others say that the tights led to the development of the mini.

Raincoats became a fashion craze for a time in the mid-sixties, when printed cotton could be waterproofed with a coating of clear plastic.

Boredom

When things wear out and have to be replaced, people want to get

> People get bored with the same clothes, or furniture, or cars.

something that is new and different. If your school has a uniform, you were probably very excited when you first wore it. How do you feel now, after several years of it?

Sexual attraction

Once people get used to seeing a part of the body, it is no longer so exciting, so people who want to look sexually attractive have to draw attention to a different bit of themselves instead.

> One way to make yourself sexually attractive is by drawing attention to an exciting part of your body.

Figure 45

> People have always used clothes as a way of saying "Look how rich and important I am."

Status symbols

If it looked as though ordinary people might be catching up, the rich could always keep ahead by moving on to a completely new fashion. They could afford to keep buying new clothes, poorer people could not.

> The more fashion changes, the more money the fashion industry makes.

The fashion industry

People have to spend money in order to keep up with new fashions.

Rebellion

The Puritans showed that they did not approve of the Cavaliers in the seventeenth century by refusing to wear the same sort of clothes.

> Breaking the rules of fashion is one way of showing that you don't care, or don't agree with other people.

Flappers in the 1920s, Teddy-boys in the 1950s, Hippies in the 1960s, Punks in the 1970s, were all using fashion to show that they did not agree with 'respectable' people.

Discuss the above statements with some of your friends. If you agree, or disagree strongly with one of them, try to find some facts to back up your opinion. You could get these from today's fashions and from fashion trends in the past. Ask older people what they remember, and what they think about some of the statements. Can you (or any of the people you talk to) think of any other reasons why fashions change?

Where does a new fashion come from?

If you study the history of fashion you will find that for hundreds of years all the new fashions came from the richest people, usually the kings and queens. Fashion nearly always changed very gradually.

Then, towards the end of the nineteenth century, professional dress designers (couturiers) in London and Paris began to lead the way. The first people to wear their clothes were their private customers, who were very rich. But ordinary people soon learned about them through newspapers and magazines. Twice a year the couturiers showed their Collections, and reporters from all over the world rushed to tell their readers what Dior, Balenciaga or Chanel was showing (figure 46).

Manufacturers adapted their designs for mass-production, and soon everybody was wearing a version of that season's "look".

Sometimes (as in 1947, when Dior presented his New Look), people had to replace all their clothes if they wanted to stay in fashion. But this did not often happen. It usually took a year or two before a new idea really caught on with the "mass-market".

Today Paris is no longer the centre of the fashion world. And the fashion world is not limited to women's clothes. Famous designers in England, America, France, Italy or Japan design for men and for women. Their clothes still cost a great deal of money, and their Collections are still reported in newspapers and magazines. But couturiers are not such a big influence as they used to be.

It all began in the 1960s and 1970s when people like Mary Quant and Barbara Hulaniki (with her Biba shops) started selling really stylish, cheap clothes. Young people loved them. Everybody under 25 years old wore them. They were so popular that soon the couturiers were being influenced by them, rather than the other way round.

Since then designers have become only one of the influences on fashion. Famous personalities, especially pop and film stars, and television series can have a big effect on fashion. Can you find some examples of these effects by collecting photos from magazines and newspapers?

Do some detective work of your own, and try to discover something about the "look" you and your friends are wearing now: when and where did it begin, and who started it?

You could start by drawing or collecting pictures of your favourite current fashion. Examine the look carefully from top to toe. Notice the shape, proportions, textures and colours. Then look back through your collection of magazines and newspapers until you find when this look

TIGHTEN YOUR BELTS!

Dior's New Look means that your waistline must shrink

Yesterday in Paris Christian Dior showed what we will all be wearing in 1947.

Figure 46

first appeared. (If you have not collected enough back-numbers, write a letter to the fashion editor of one of the magazines or newspapers asking if they can help you.)

How long did it take before you and your friends started wearing this particular look? Can you remember seeing pictures of it when it first appeared? What did you think of it then?

A famous fashion historian called James Laver had a theory about this.

People think a fashion is:

Indecent ......10 years before its time
Shameless ...5 years before its time
Daring ....1 year before its time
Smart ....when it is in fashion
Dowdy ....1 year after its time
Ugly ....10 years after its time
Ridiculous ...20 years after its time
Amusing .....30 years after its time
Quaint ....50 years after its time
Charming ....70 years after its time
Romantic .....100 years after its time
Beautiful .....150 years after its time

Of course, when James Laver wrote this, fashions changed much more slowly than they do today. But do you think his general idea was right?

Discuss it with people who are old enough to have seen lots of different fashions come and go. If you agree with the general idea, could you re-write the table, making the number of years more up-to-date?

Fashion and proportion

Do you think this "see-saw" theory (figure 47) has always been true? Is it true of men's fashion, as well as women's? Do you think it is true of fashion today?

Decide for yourself by studying the fashions of different periods in the past, and the fashions of the last few years. If you agree with the theory, try using it to forecast what the next fashionable shape will be.

Fashion and the human body

If clothes really did give clues about what was inside them, time-travellers from outer space would take back some strange ideas about the human body. For example, what sort of bodies do you think would fit naturally into the clothes in figures 49–51? Figure 48 shows the outline of the body that would fit into the fashion shape illustrated.

Women's fashion is rather like a see-saw. Once a fashionable shape starts to grow, it goes on growing until it can't grow anymore. Then it either collapses, like a pricked balloon, or it gradually shrivels away and something else starts to grow instead.

Figure 47 The changing shapes of trousers and tops between the 1930s and 1970s.

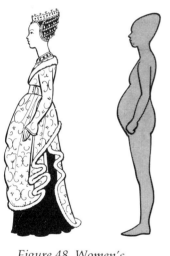

Figure 48 Women's fashion in 1470.

Figure 50 Men's fashion in 1560.

Figure 49 Women's fashion in 1585.

Figure 51 Women's fashion in 1860.

People never seem to be satisfied with the bodies nature gave them. Throughout history they have padded themselves out, or squeezed themselves in. Some fashions must have been horribly uncomfortable; others certainly damaged their health. But fashion always came first. In the twentieth century things began to improve, and fashion became much more safe and comfortable – or did it (figure 52)?

Rock Star blames fashion

"Platform-soled shoes were the cause of my injury" said the pop star

New Fashion a health risk?

"Mini-skirts are putting young girls at risk" said Dr Jones, of

TIGHT JEANS CAN DAMAGE YOUR PROSPECTS!

Recent tests have shown that young men who constantly wear very tight jeans have a lower sperm count than their less fashion-conscious friends.

Figure 52

How do you rate today's fashions as far as comfort and safety are concerned?

Fashion and you

Are you a fashion leader, or a follower? Are you (or would you like to be) one of the first people in your group to start wearing a new fashion? If so, is it because
you like to stand out from the crowd?
you are more interested in fashion than your friends are?
your family does not mind you looking "different"?
or another reason?
  Or are you one of the last people in your group to change your style? If so, is it because
people might stare, and you would feel embarrassed?
you do not want to "follow the herd". You want to be sure a fashion is right for you before you change?
you cannot afford to change your style as often as you would like?
your family makes it difficult for you?
or another reason?

With a group of friends, discuss your feelings about fashion.
When did you start getting interested in it?
How important is fashion to you now?
Who is the best-dressed person you know: in your own age-group;
in an older age-group? What is it about these people that you
admire most?

Compare notes about where you get your fashion ideas from:
fashion magazines, newspapers, shop-windows, famous people,
TV, films, catalogues, adverts, other people you see around you. Or
do your ideas come from your own imagination?

Fitting into fashion

Most fashions are designed with an ideal person in mind. Most of the
people who wear those fashions are not "ideal".

Before the 1970s, when fashion was like a uniform, life could be very
difficult for some people. Since then, things have become much easier.
There usually seem to be several "looks" to choose from, so everyone
can wear something that suits them. Provided, of course, they know
what to choose.

The first step to knowing what to choose is to *know yourself* (figure
53). Everyone has good points and bad points. Do you really know
what yours are?

If you are like most people of your age, you probably know all your
bad points by heart, and you think everybody else knows them as
well. You may even spend so much time worrying about your bad
points that you never discover all your *good* points.

Get together with one or two friends and make really honest lists
of your own, and one another's, good and bad points.

When you have all finished, compare your own list with the ones
your friends have made about you. Did they mention any good
points that were not on your own list? Were there any bad points on
your own list that your friends had not noticed?

Look at the list of bad points. Discuss with your friends what you
could do about them. Could a new haircut, or a better diet, or some
exercise improve any of them? If not, forget about them. They are
probably not nearly as noticeable as you imagine.

Figure 53

Make people notice your good points

Look at figure 54. What do you notice first?

Figure 54

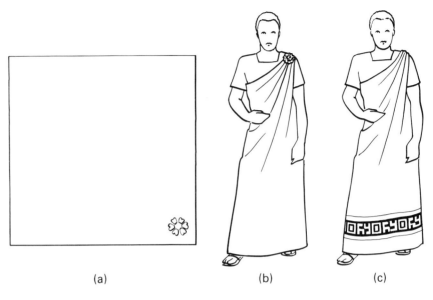

(a)   (b)   (c)

You can draw people's attention away from your bad points if you have something really interesting or brightly coloured somewhere else.

What advice would you give to the people in figure 55, using today's fashions?

Figure 55

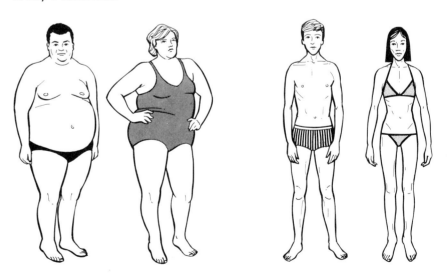

Look bigger . . . Look smaller . . .

You can make yourself look taller or shorter, fatter or thinner, if you know how to fool the eye (figure 56).

Figure 56

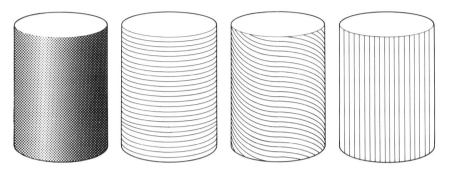

Colour, texture, line, shape, proportion can all change the way you look. Can you see how they make the figures in figure 57 look different?

Figure 57

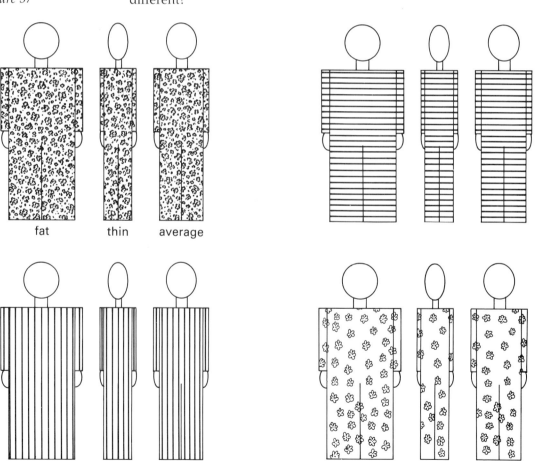

fat   thin   average

Experiment with fashion on your own figure shape. Get someone to take some black-and-white photographs of you (in swimwear) and have the film developed (not printed). Then project the negative, as though it was a slide, on to a piece of white paper and draw around it, several times. Draw clothes in different styles, proportions and colours onto the shape and see the different effects.

Make an appointment to visit some of your local fashion shops with a friend, at a time when they are not too busy, and ask them to help you choose a complete outfit for a particular occasion. For example: an interview; a day out in the country; a date; a walk in the park. (If you or your teacher explain that this is part of a school course, you will find that most retailers will be pleased to help you.)

Work out what each outfit cost and, if you can, arrange to be photographed in each of them.

You could share this experience with other pupils if you put up a display of your photographs. Perhaps you could make it into a regular fashion feature.

Choose a period when fashion changed suddenly, for example 1790, 1918, 1940, 1947, 1960. Find out whether anything else changed at about the same time – transport, houses, furniture, music, entertainment.

What do the history books tell you about that time? Was there a great political change, a war, or a change in people's way of life? Do you think any of these things caused the sudden change in fashion?

Study recent issues of high-fashion magazines and find out who today's really important designers are. Which of them have the biggest influence on the clothes that are sold in the High Street?

Collect pictures of these designers' work, and examples of the High Street fashions that they have inspired. (Or you may find that it is the other way round – they may have got some of their ideas from "street fashion").

Choose one or two designers whose work you like best, and find out as much as you can about them.

Practise looking at fashion. Flip through some of your favourite magazines for a few minutes, until you come across an outfit that you really like. Quickly shut the magazine, get out a pencil and paper and draw the outfit from memory.

Pass your drawing and the magazine picture to a friend and ask him or her to compare the two. How well had you remembered the picture? Do this as often as you can, and you will find it does wonders for your fashion sense.

SEE ALSO

Advertising, and *Shopping* for information about how manufacturers and retailers try to persuade you to buy things. *Man-made fibres* for more about ways in which inventions have influenced fashion.

FADS: Fashion design and figure appreciation. Published by the Advisory Unit (was AUCBE), (address on page 197) in 1986. This is a computer program which enables you to design clothes for your own figure.

Four Hundred Years of Fashion (Victoria & Albert Museum/Collins). (The catalogue of the Costume Court at the V & A – very well illustrated, with interesting articles by experts on the Museum's staff.)
Everyday Fashions of the Twenties, as featured in Sears and Other Catalogues, by Stella Blum (Dover).
Dressing and Undressing for the Beach, by Irina Lindsay (Ian Henry 1983).
In Fashion, by Prudence Glyn and Madeleine Ginsburg (Allen & Unwin 1978).
Bruce Oldfield's Season, (Pan Books) – a season behind-the-scenes in a couture house.
A Visual History of Costume, series (B T Batsford).
The Way to Wear 'Em – 150 Years of Punch on Fashion, by Christina Walkley (Peter Owen).
McDowell's Dictionary of Twentieth Century Fashion, by Colin McDowell (Frederick Muller).
The Language of Clothes, by Alison Lurie.

Fibres

Collect fabric scraps; an assortment of different yarns (machine thread, knitting yarn, threads pulled out of fabric, and so on); pins; a magnifying glass or low-power microscope.

Take a scrap of fabric, and gently pull it apart. Then take one of the threads and carefully untwist it until *it* falls apart. Those tiny, hair-like strands you are left with are the fibres. Small though they are, these fibres have given the fabric most of its properties.

Figure 58 Surface view of human hair magnified 3500 times

Figure 59 Cross-section and surface view of fibres of:
(a) acetate,
(b) acrylic,
continued overleaf

Look around your class at the different types of hair you can see. Just like hairs, fibres come in all sorts of different lengths, thicknesses and shapes. Some are springy and wiry, others are soft and bendy. If fibres are magnified, you can see even more differences between them. A magnified hair looks like figure 58 but other fibres look different (figure 59). All these differences have an important effect on the yarns and fabrics that are made from the fibres.

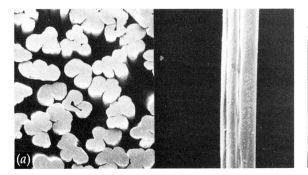
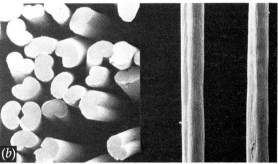

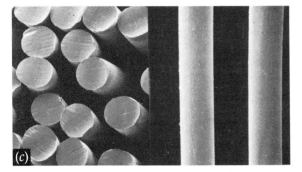
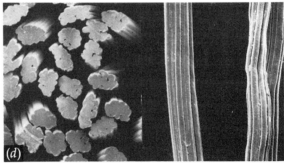

Figure 59 continued
(c) *polyester,*
(d) *viscose, magnified*
1700 times.

> Fibres that are crimped like this ᴍᴍᴍ, can be pulled out straight _____. When they are released, they will spring back to their original shape. These crimped fibres will make more elastic yarns and fabrics than straight ones.

> The longer the fibres, the smoother the yarns and fabrics made from them will be. The shorter the fibre, the fuzzier the yarns and fabrics will be.

> Straight, smooth, shiny fibres will make smooth shiny yarns and fabrics.

You can find out if these statements are true by examining some fabrics.

Collect some different types of fabric (smooth, rough, shiny) and cut a sample of each, about 10 cm square. Find out which fabric is the most elastic by pulling it, along the threads, in both directions.

Pull a thread from each fabric and very gently remove some fibres from each of them as in figure 60 (be careful not to break the fibres as you do this). You may find it easier if you untwist the thread and then use two pins to tease the fibres.

Compare the lengths of the fibres. Which fabric has the longest fibres? Which has the shortest? Look at the fibres under a magnifying glass. Are some smoother than others? Are some of them straighter? Which fabric has the straightest fibres? The most wavy fibres?

Are the three statements above true?

Figure 60 Separating fibres.

Figure 61 A reel of continuous filament yarn.

Figure 62 A reel of staple yarn.

Staple and filament fibres

If you were to unwind all the thread on the reel in figure 61, you would find that it is over 2 km long. If you could then separate the fibres, you would find that there are only about six of them, and each one would be over 2 km long.

Very long fibres like these are called *filaments*, or *filament fibres*. You can find out more about them on pages 94, 133, 138 and 192.

The thread on the reel in figure 62 is also about 2 km long. But if you were to separate these fibres you would find that there are thousands of them, and they are each about 6 mm long.

Short fibres like these are called *staple fibres*, and they can be anything from 3 mm to 500 mm long. The hairs on your head are staple fibres. So are the hairs on your dog or cat. You can find out more about staple fibres on pages 90, 99 and 190.

SEE ALSO

Choosing fabrics for more about the properties and characteristics of fabrics.
Fibres from animals, Fibres from plants, Man-made fibres for information about different types of fibres.
"Non-woven" fabrics, Yarns to find out what happens to fibres.
Properties of fibres chart for information about different types of fibre.

Fibres from animals

Send for the International Wool Secretariat Education Pack, and their 50 year review and booklet about the International Wool Secretariat Development Centre (address on page 199).
Send for *Silk* (Entomology Leaflet No. 7) from the Natural History Museum.
Collect samples of raw fleece and silk; samples of yarns and fabrics made from different animal fibres. (The Handweavers' Studio and Gallery will sell very small quantities; address on page 198.)

Many animals (apart from ones like lizards and frogs) grow fibres. You do, and so does your dog, your cat and your rabbit. Some insects make fibres – spiders used them for their webs, and moths and butterflies make their cocoons from them.

Not all animal fibres can be used for making fabrics. Cows, Siamese cats and Labrador dogs, for example, have hairs that are too short and stiff, but you can probably think of others whose hair could easily be made into cloth. Animals like poodles or Persian cats, however, are not big enough to grow much hair. You would need millions and millions of them and they would be too expensive to feed.

Wool

What is needed is an animal that is cheap to feed, that grows lots of hair, and is tame enough to let us take that hair from it. The only animal that has all these qualities is the sheep, and ever since prehistoric times people have used its fleece to make cloth. We call the fibres that we get from the sheep *wool*.

Figure 63 tells how you might make yarn from fleece.

Some facts about wool

• Figure 64 shows a wool fibre through a microscope (magnified many times). Just like the hairs that grow on your body, it is covered with tiny scales that overlap, rather like roof-tiles. Different types of animal hair have their scales arranged differently; not all wool fibres look exactly the same under the microscope. As you can see, the scales stick out slightly.
• Wool fibres have a natural permanent wave or *crimp*. This means that they are very elastic. If they are stretched or crushed, they will always bounce back to their original size and shape.

HOW TO MAKE A YARN FROM WOOL

① First catch your sheep...

Shear it. You can use hand or power-clippers.

② Sort out the different parts of the fleece. The best wool grows on the sides and shoulders of the sheep.

Wash the wool in detergent, to remove dirt, grease, sweat, seeds and other vegetable matter. This is called SCOURING.

③ Leave the bowl of water to cool. Skim off the grease (LANOLIN) which floats to the top, and use it for making hand-cream.

④ When the fibres are dry, gently tease them apart with dog-brushes until they make a thin filmy web. This process is called CARDING. The web is called a CARD SLIVER.

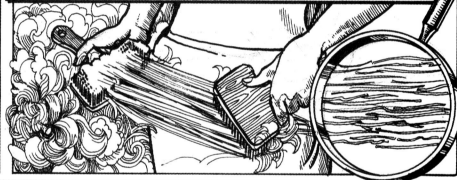

EITHER ⑤ Separate the sliver into several groups, like soft ropes (ROVINGS) about the same thickness as your finger.

Gently pull the rovings, and twist (SPIN) them to make WOOLLEN YARN.

OR ⑥ Comb the sliver carefully. Make sure that there are no tangles — the fibres should lie parallel to each other.

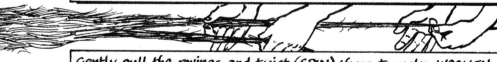

Gently draw out the combed sliver and twist (SPIN) it to make a WORSTED YARN.

Figure 63

Figure 64 Cross-section (magnified 300 times) and surface view (magnified 1500 times) of wool fibres.

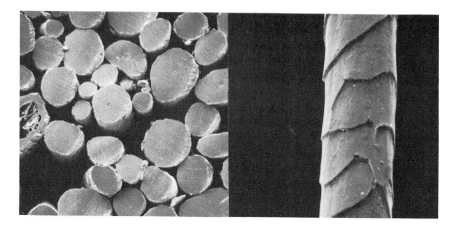

- What makes sheep particularly useful is that, just like dogs and people, there are different breeds, which each grow different kinds of fleece. You can see the different lengths, and also the varying amounts of crimp in different fleece samples. If you feel them you will also notice that some are very fine and soft, while others are thicker and feel quite harsh. This makes wool a very versatile fibre. It can be made into anything from a hard-wearing carpet to a delicate shawl for a baby.
- The scales on its fibres give wool a property that is both an advantage and a disadvantage. The property is called *felting*. It happens if wool yarns or fabrics are treated roughly when they are hot and wet, for example during machine washing. The scales lock together, which makes the fibres tangle into a hard, shrunken mat. When this is done on purpose, it makes a useful fabric called *felt*. When it happens accidentally, the item is ruined. Wool can now be treated to make it shrink-resistant (see page 112–3, and the International Wool Secretariat Education Pack.)

When natural protein fibres get damp, they feel *warmer*.

- Wool fibres are made of a protein called *keratin*. Therefore, wool is a *natural protein fibre*. (Your hair and fingernails are keratin. So are animal horns and hooves. Burning hair smells the same as burning nail-clippings.)
- Other animals (camels, the angora rabbit, and certain breeds of goat, for example) are also kept for their hair, some of which makes especially beautiful cloth. But it is much more expensive to produce than wool, so you are unlikely to find much of it in your local shops. Only items made from wool are allowed to carry the "woolmark" label shown in figure 65.

Get together with a group of friends and make a list of things you own that are made of wool. (Check the labels, to be sure they *are* wool.)

Discuss what they are like to use, wear and care for. Ask your family and neighbours, too. Find out what they like and do not like about wool. Make a list of what you think are the properties of wool.

Then look up wool in some of your reference books, and on the chart on page 148. Were you right about its properties? Use your reference books to find out why wool has these properties. Do any other fibres have some of the same properties?

Try to get some raw fleece (as it comes from the sheep). Measure its *staple length* (see page 98). Feel it and smell it, then wash some of it carefully in warm soapy water. Try making it into yarn (see page 191). Which is easier – the washed or the unwashed fleece?

Make a wool scrapbook: collect pictures of things made from wool: furnishings, crafts, fashions, and so on; collect as many different wool fabrics and yarns as you can. If you know the price, put that in as well. (Test them to make sure they really are wool before you put them in the scrapbook – you can find out how to do this on pages 176–8.

Visit a carpet shop; a knitting shop; a fabric shop; a craft shop; some clothes shops. Look at the labels, to find out how many things made from wool are on sale. Look at the price tags.

Find things that look the same, but are not made from wool. How much do they cost?

Imagine you were serving in one of those shops: how would you persuade a customer to buy something made from wool rather than from another fibre?

If the customer bought the item made from wool, what advice would you give about looking after it?

Find out what is meant by "Botany wool" and "Lambswool". Try to find some fabrics, or items, made from these two types of wool, and from *woollen* and *worsted* yarns as well.

CERTIFICATION TRADE MARK
PURE NEW WOOL

Figure 65 This is the "woolmark" label. Find out what it means and when it can and cannot be used.

Look for fabrics or yarns made from different animal hair. (They will be called, for example, Cashmere, Alpaca, Camelhair, Mohair, Angora.) Find out the name of the animal and the part of the world they came from.

How much do they cost to buy? Feel them. Do you think they are worth the money?

HOW TO MAKE SILK YARNS

① You will need: some BOMBYX MORI and a mulberry tree...

Wait until the moth starts laying eggs.

② When you notice grubs (SILK WORMS) hatching out of the eggs, give them some fresh mulberry leaves to eat.

MULB LEAV

If you feed them with plenty of fresh leaves for another 35 days, they will grow 10,000 times heavier than when they hatched – like little bags of liquid silk.

③ Put some twigs in their cage and watch them spin their cocoons (which will take them about two days, non-stop). By the time they have finished, they will each have wound a mile of silk around themselves.

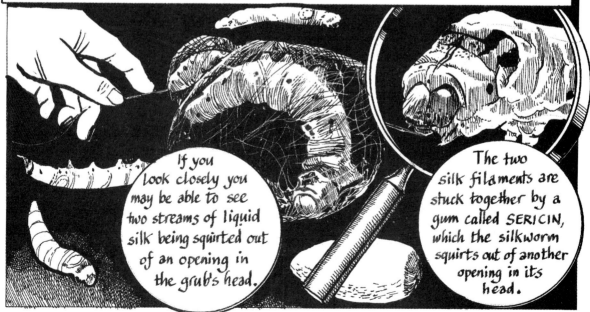

If you look closely you may be able to see two streams of liquid silk being squirted out of an opening in the grub's head.

The two silk filaments are stuck together by a gum called SERICIN, which the silkworm squirts out of another opening in its head.

Figure 66

4. Now harden your heart. Put the cocoons into a bath of boiling water, to kill the chrysalis inside.

If you let them grow into moths, they will eat their way out of the cocoons: just like slicing down a reel of sewing thread with a razor blade — you will be left with thousands of short scraps instead of one long thread.

5. When the water is cool enough, take several cocoons and brush them, to find the ends of the threads.

Pull gently, and wind the skeins on to a reel. This is very difficult — you will need a lot of practice to do it properly.

6. You now have a skein of raw silk, which looks rather dull. If you want your silk to be smooth and shiny, you must wash off the gum (SERICIN)

MILD ALKALI

7. Twist about four filaments together to make Thrown Silk Yarn.

Figure 66 continued

Silk

Five thousand years ago the Chinese discovered how to unwind the cocoons of a particular moth (*Bombyx mori*) and how to use the long, smooth fibres for making cloth. This cloth was so beautiful that people travelled from all over the world to buy it. It was so precious that it cost more than if it had been made from pure gold thread.

The Chinese kept the secret of their moth for more than three thousand years, but eventually it was "leaked" to another country. Today there are silk farms all over the world, where *Bombyx mori* are reared and the silk is made into an enormous variety of luxury fabrics. There is a silk farm in England, which traditionally has provided silk for Royal wedding dresses.

Although you can now buy some quite cheap silk clothes, not many people own more than one or two items made from pure silk. And you are not likely to make anything from silk until you are an experienced craftsperson. Some silk fabrics can be difficult to work with, and it is too expensive to risk making mistakes. But it is still important for you to know about silk, because it will help you to understand the man-made fibres we use today (see page 133).

Figure 66 shows how you might make silk yarn.

Some facts about silk

A dry silk thread is stronger than a steel thread of the same thickness. During the Second World War, parachutes were made from silk.

● Short, broken pieces of silk filament are not thrown away. They are degummed, and then carded and spun into yarn, in much the same way as wool and cotton yarns are made. Silk yarns made like this are called *spun silk*.

● You may come across fabric or yarn that is labelled *Wild silk* or *Tussah silk*. This comes from the cocoon of a different type of silk-moth (*Antherea mylitta*), which feeds on oak-leaves. Because it is a wild moth, it is difficult to kill all the chrysalises before they hatch out, so wild silk is nearly always *spun* into yarn. If you can examine a wild silk fibre, you will notice that it is not so smooth and even as cultivated silk.

● When it is degummed silk weighs less, which can mean higher prices, or less profit for the manufacturer.

To keep the price down, silk fabric is sometimes *weighted* by being put in a bath of tin-phosphate-silicate salts. The salts are absorbed into the fabric, which makes up the weight lost by degumming. If you are able to examine a piece of weighted silk fabric, you will notice that it crushes and wrinkles more easily than pure silk.

● Figure 67 shows degummed silk fibres under a microscope (magnified many times). Notice that, although they are very smooth, they are not round, as you might expect.

Figure 67 Cross-section and surface view of silk fibres, magnified 1500 times.

How easy is it to buy silk? Visit your local shops and find out whether any of them sells silk yarns, silk fabrics, silk threads or items made from silk. Do not just look at them – there are a lot of imitation silks that might mislead you. Look at the labels: the words "silk" or "pure silk" should be there somewhere.

Find out how much silk fabrics and yarns cost to buy. Try to collect an example of each of these silk fabrics: chiffon, organza, taffeta, satin, shantung, crepe, jersey, shot silk, grosgrain, wild silk.

Do you, or your family, or friends and neighbours have any things made from silk? Perhaps someone has a pure silk sari. Ask them about the properties of their silk fabrics.

Use your reference books and the chart on page 148 to find out more about the properties of silk. Find out why people who can afford it like it so much for things like underclothes and sheets.

Silk is not an "easy-care" fibre. Try to find out why.

See if you can borrow some silk yarns, or fabrics, or items made from silk, and bring them to school. Examine them carefully. Can you tell which have been made from *thrown* (continuous filament) yarns and which from *spun* yarns? Are any of them made from wild (tussah) silk?

Collect some things made from other fibres that look and feel "silky". Compare the real thing and the imitation. Can you tell the difference? If you could afford it, would you choose real silk rather than an imitation?

If you are experimenting with dyes during your course, try to put some silk fabric samples in the dyebaths as well. Compare the colours you get on the silk with the colours you get on other fabrics.

SEE ALSO

Man-made fibres to see how scientists tried to copy the silk worm.
"Non-woven" fabrics, for information about felt.
Properties of fibres chart.
Tests for help with identifying fibres.
Yarns to see how fibres are made into yarns.

If you can, visit the International Wool Secretariat Development Centre (by appointment) – address on page 199.

The Weaving, Spinning and Dyeing Book, by Rachel Brown (Routledge and Kegan Paul).
Wool; by H S Bell (Pitman).
Textiles: Properties and Behaviour in Clothing Use, by Edward Miller (B T Batsford Ltd).
Handbook of Textiles, by A M Collier (Wheaton).
Textiles by N Hollen, J Saddler and A L Langford (Collier Macmillan Ltd).

KEY WORDS
Crimp the sheep's natural wave, which can vary from almost straight to very tight, according to the breed.
Felting the matting together of wool fibres, which causes a fabric to shrink and harden.
Staple length the natural length of a fibre.

Fibres from plants

Collect samples of fabrics and yarns made from cotton, linen, jute.

Fibres from plants are made mostly of cellulose. They are therefore known as *natural cellulosic fibres*.

Have you ever eaten stringy celery, rhubarb, or runner beans? If you have, you will know that some plants have quite tough fibres in their stems, or in the casings round their seeds.

Linen

People have been making yarns from plant fibres for many thousands of years. Pieces of fabric made from plant fibres were found in prehistoric sites in Switzerland. When archaeologists explored Egyptian tombs they found that the mummies were wrapped in similar fabrics.

These fabrics are believed to have been made from a plant that belongs to a family called *linus*. This particular plant is known as flax: the cloth that is made from it is called *linen*.

Figure 68 shows how you could make yarns from flax plants.

Some facts about linen

- Fully-grown flax plants are about 1 m tall.
- The average length of a flax fibre is 500 mm.
- Figure 69 shows flax fibres through a microscope. They are easy to recognise because of the lines that run across them, rather like a bamboo cane.

  One of the characteristics of a linen fabric is its slight sheen. This is because the fibres are *polygonal* (many-sided), and reflect the light.

- The two different types of linen yarn described in figure 68 have some different properties:

  Line yarn is finer, smoother, more lustrous, cooler, more durable, stronger, less absorbent, and faster drying.

HOW TO MAKE YARNS FROM FLAX PLANTS

① You will need; one or more fully grown flax plants; pull them up, roots and all.

Cut off the roots, then keep the stems wet, until they have rotted (this is called RETTING).

② Crush the stems, until all the woody bits have been separated from the fibres.

This is called SCUTCHING.

③ Carefully comb the fibres, just as though you were combing your hair.
When you have done this, they should look smooth and tidy, like long blond hair.
This process is called HACKLING. It turns the bunches of fibre into a sliver.

A lot of short fibres will be combed out. Don't throw these away.

④ Pull gently, letting the fibres slide over one another until the sliver is the thickness you want.

Twist the sliver to make a smooth line yarn.

⑤ gather up all the short fibres. Use wire brushes to tease them apart into a carded web.

CARDED SLIVERS

⑥ Gently pull the sliver, letting the fibres slide over each other, until it is the thickness you want.

Twist (SPIN) the sliver to make a TOW YARN.

Figure 68

Figure 69 Cross-section and surface view of linen fibres, magnified 1500 times.

Uses of line and tow yarn

Line	*Tow*
batiste	sheeting
cambric	towelling
handkerchiefs	suiting
damask	
suiting	

● Today flax is grown in the USSR, some European countries, and Ireland. They grow it in America, Australia and New Zealand too, but not for the fibres. They extract linseed oil from the seeds.

● Have you noticed that, although very few people buy pure linen these days, the words "bed-linen" and "table-linen" are still used?

Look in your local shops to find out whether they sell any linen. (Look at the labels – "pure linen" or "Irish linen" should be there somewhere.)

If you find fabric or items made from linen, notice the price, and compare it with something similar that is made from a different fibre.

In the 1950s it became possible to make fabrics that looked like linen, but they did not crease so badly, were much cheaper, and not so flammable. Try to get hold of a piece of real linen and a piece of "linen-look" fabric. Examine them carefully. What differences do you notice?

Look at the tea-towels you use at home and in school. Are they made of cotton or linen? If you can find an example of each type, use them for drying some glassware and compare the results.

Linen used to be a very popular fabric for sheets, pillowcases, tablecloths, and clothing. Use your reference books and the chart on page 148 to find out why, and why it is not used so much now. Find out how much a pure linen sheet costs today.

When you are looking for linen, you may find it mixed with other fibres. Make a note of these fibres (and the *proportions* in which they are used) and examine the fabric or yarn carefully.

If it is mostly linen (e.g. 75% linen; 25% polyester), try to work out why the other fibres have been added. If it is mostly other fibres (e.g. 75% viscose; 25% linen), try to work out what the linen is there for.

Other plant fibres

Flax is not the only plant with useful fibres in its stem. Jute, hemp and ramie have been used for thousands of years for things like sacks, ropes, twine and, more recently, backing for carpets and lino.

Next time you are in a greengrocer's, look for a coconut and examine it carefully. You may be able to see traces of the coarse fibres that covered it. Go to a carpet shop and you may find those fibres, used to make a coir mat. You may also find mats or carpets made from sisal. This fibre comes from the leaves of the sisal plant.

Try making your own yarns from plant fibres. Here are some ideas to start you off: leaves with strong-looking veins; nettles; celery; rhubarb;, rose-bay willowherb or the long silken tassels on heads of sweetcorn.

Experiment to find the best way of removing the fibres from the plants. Try soaking them in cold water, or warm water. Try boiling or simmering them.

If you find that some of the fibres are easier, or more difficult to spin into yarn, try to work out why this is. What properties must a fibre have, if it is going to be useful for making textiles?

Cotton

Some plants (like the dandelion) use fibres to help their seeds to float through the air. Another plant that spreads its seeds like this is the cotton plant.

Five thousand years ago the people of India began to use these fibres for making yarns and fabrics. Cotton proved so popular that other countries with the same sort of climate began growing the plant, and today more than 16 million tons of cotton fibre are produced every year.

Figure 70 shows how you could make yarns from cotton plants.

Some facts about cotton

• Each cotton boll contains about 30 hard seeds, each about the same size as a pea. The boll is so fluffy because each seed has more than 5000 fibres growing over it.

• Figure 71 shows cotton fibres magnified many times. At first glance, cotton fibres look rather like twisted ribbons. But if you look carefully at figure 71, you will see that they are really tiny collapsed tubes, rather like bicycle inner-tubes that have had all the air let out. When the cotton boll is still on the plant, the fibres are round. They collapse because, like any plant, they dry out once they have been picked.

Figure 71 Cross-section and surface view of cotton fibres, magnified 1700 times.

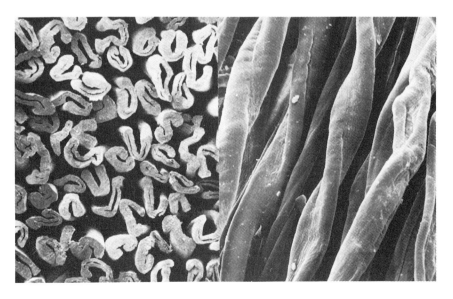

• Because cotton fibres are flat and twisted, they do not reflect the light, so cotton yarns and fabrics normally look rather dull. To give cotton a sheen (or lustre), the fibres need to be "pumped up" so that they lose their twist. (You can find out more about this on pages 108–9.)

HOW TO MAKE YARNS FROM COTTON

① You will need: one or more cotton bushes.

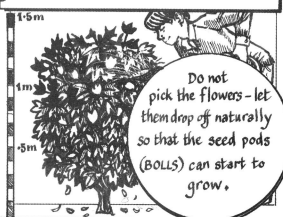

Do not pick the flowers – let them drop off naturally so that the seed pods (BOLLS) can start to grow.

② Watch the bolls carefully...

Pick the bolls once they are fully opened.

③ Remove any pieces of twig or leaves, then scrape the fibres off the seeds. This is called GINNING.

Throw away the leaves and twigs. Put the seeds in a safe place until you have read page 134...

COTTON   LINTERS

④ If your cotton fibres are short (up to about 35mm), tease them apart to make a carded web.

Gently stretch (DRAW) the carded web and twist (SPIN) it into CARDED cotton yarn...

⑤ If your fibres are mostly long (35–65 mm), comb them carefully and then spin them into COMBED cotton yarn.

Keep any very short fibres that are combed out...

⑥ If your fibres are very short (less than 25mm), tease them apart into a web.

Divide the web into separate strands (ROVINGS) and very gently stretch (DRAW) them until they are the thickness you want. Then twist (SPIN) them into CONDENSER SPUN Cotton Yarn.

Figure 70

- Cotton fibres, like sheep's wool, vary quite a lot. The climate, the way it is grown, and the plant itself can all affect the length and fineness of the cotton fibres.

The best fibres are grown in the West Indies and are called *Sea Island cotton*: they are very white, long and fine, and make beautiful smooth cloth.

Egyptian cotton is the next best. It is not quite so fine, or white, but it is still considered to be very high quality.

Ordinary cotton has shorter (25–30 mm), coarser fibres: it is known as the American type. Almost three-quarters of the world's cotton comes in this group.

The poorest cotton fibres are very short (20–25 mm), coarse, and a creamy colour. Most of this comes from India and other Asian countries, and it has the advantage of being very cheap. Fabrics made from these fibres have become very popular since the "ethnic look" came into fashion.

How much cotton do you and your family use in your daily life? It may be more (or less) than you think.

Find out by making a list (on your own, with a group or as a class) of all the cotton items you and your family use.

Look at things like dusters and bath-mats as well as clothing and furnishings. If you find that some items are made from other fibres as well as cotton, make a note of the numbers. For example, if you find 8 pairs of underpants and 6 of them are cotton, you could write it as a fraction (6/8) or a percentage (75%).

When the list is complete, decide which items are most often made from cotton. Are there any items which always seem to be made of cotton? If so, does this give you any clues about some of the properties of cotton? Think about your own experience with those items – using them, washing and drying them.

What have you noticed about the properties of your cotton fabrics? How do they compare with things made from other fibres? What do you think are their advantages, and disadvantages?

Compare your ideas with information about cotton in your reference books, and in the chart on page 148.

Look in the shops, and in mail-order catalogues, for cotton fabrics and yarns, and items made from cotton.

How many things do you find that are made from 100% cotton? How much do they cost? Are there many things on sale that are made from cotton mixed with another fibre? Why do you think this is? (How much do they cost?)

Collect samples of as many different cotton fabrics and yarns as you can. Examine them carefully and see if you can work out which type of cotton yarn they are made from. Try to find an example of Sea Island or Egyptian cotton fabric, to compare with the rest of your collection.

Imagine you could only use cotton for your clothes, furnishings and craft-work.

How comfortable would you be? How would you keep warm, cool or dry? Would you be able to find enough materials for your craft? Would you have to change your designs in any way?

Try one of these: design a winter outfit; or a knitted or embroidered wall-hanging; or a woven rug; all to be made from 100% cotton.

What do you think cotton-wool is made from? Have a guess, then look at the label to find out.

SEE ALSO

Finishing fabrics for information about some of the ways in which the properties of fibres can be altered.
Mixtures and blends for some reasons why different fibres are mixed together.
Properties of fibres chart for more information about the properties of linen and cotton.

The Weaving, Spinning and Dyeing Book, by Rachel Brown (Routledge and Kegan Paul).
Textiles; Properties and Behaviour in Clothing Use, by Edward Miller (B T Batsford Ltd).
Handbook of Textiles, by A M Collier (Wheaton).
Textiles, by N Hollen, J Saddler and A L Langford (Collier Macmillan Ltd).

KEY WORDS

Natural cellulosic fibres fibres that come from plants, and are used in their natural state.
Regenerated cellulosic fibres fibres made from cellulose that has been turned into a liquid and then re-made into fibres. (See page 134.)

Picture 3   *See text on pages 28–9.*

Picture 4   See text on page 30.

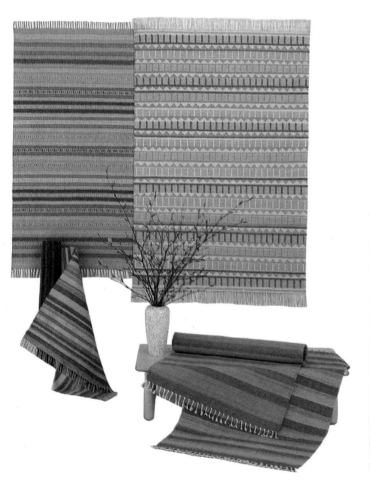

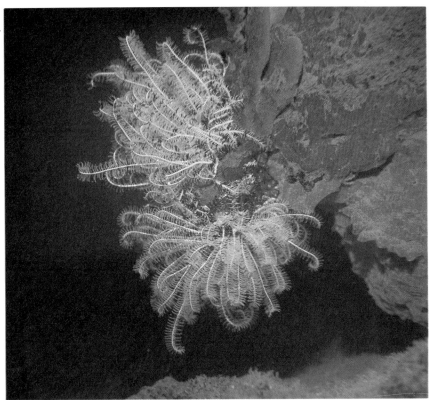

a

b

Picture 6 *See text on pages 107–117. Some fabrics with different finishes.*

Picture 7 *See text on pages 194–5. Many different novelty yarns are available; this is just a sample.*

Finishing fabrics

Collect about 1 m of loom-state cotton fabric (unbleached calico is probably the easiest to find).
Rubber gloves; china or glass bowls; 3% hydrogen peroxide solution; 18–25% sodium hydroxide (caustic soda) solution; borax and boric acid; an electric razor; a fine wire brush; goggles (for eye protection); a small (approx. 7 cm × 7 cm) piece of wood or hardboard; piece of wire or a skewer; oven gloves; water-repellent and stain-repellent sprays.

When a piece of fabric comes off the loom or knitting machine, it is called *loom-state* or *grey goods*, and it may look very dingy and unattractive. By the time it reaches you, the same fabric can look and feel quite different. This is because it may have been through a series of processes which have finished off the work done by the spinners, weavers or knitters.

In picture 6, on the opposite page, you can see some examples of fabrics that have been changed by different finishing processes.

Finishes can be divided into three main groups:

Basic finishes, which get the fabric ready for the next stages.

Aesthetic finishes which help to give the fabric the right look, feel and drape.

Performance finishes, which give the fabric extra useful properties, or improve some of the properties it already has.

Some of these finishes will be *permanent* – they will last as long as the fabric does. Some will be *temporary* – they will disappear once the fabric has been washed or cleaned. Some will be *durable* – they will last longer than temporary finishes, but will eventually wear out. They can often be damaged if washing or cleaning instructions are not followed carefully. A few will be *renewable* – you will be able to replace them yourself, or pay a dry-cleaner to do it.

Finishing fabrics is a very complicated business which needs a great deal of expertise, and much expensive equipment. Some fabric manufacturers do their own finishing, but most of them send their grey-goods to factories that specialise in finishing.

The table on pages 108–113 contains information about some of the most common finishes. If you need more detail, you will find it in the books on pages 106 and 117.

Table of common finishing processes

Name of finish	Purpose	When done	Fibres used on	How it is done
Basic finishes				
Cleaning [kiering (cotton); scouring (wool); degumming (silk)]	To remove: size or starch; chemicals left on man-made fibres; dirt and grease; sericin from silk.	Usually after weaving	Mostly natural fibres	Washing, boiling, soaking in solvent
Bleaching	To clean and whiten grey-goods	Before or after fabric is made	Cellulosics; wool (sometimes); man-made fibres (sometimes)	Soaking in chemical (different bleaches used for different fibres)
Beetling	To produce smoother, more lustrous fabric	After other finishing processes	Linen (sometimes cotton)	Fabric is pounded with wooden blocks (for up to three days)
Tentering (or stentering)	To pull fabric back into shape after construction and finishing	One of the final finishing processes. Usually done when fabric is wet or damp.	All	Selvedges are gripped by tiny pins or clips. Fabric is stretched into shape and held while it dries.
Singeing	To make fabric smoother	After cleaning and bleaching	Mainly cotton, some smooth wools	Dry fabric is passed very quickly over gas flame.
Aesthetic Finishes				
Shearing, cropping	Trim pile of raised fabrics, or create smooth surface	After basic finishing	Most	Fabric is passed through machine with revolving blades
Brushing, napping	To make fabric feel softer and warmer, look different	One of the last finishing processes	Most	Fabric is brushed with fine wire brushes.
Mercerising	To make cotton more lustrous	After spinning or fabric construction, before dyeing	Only cellulosic yarns and fabrics	Yarns or fabrics (stretched tight) are soaked in concentrated sodium hydroxide (caustic soda) solution

Effect it has	Other effects	Durability	Visibility	Common uses/ Trade names
Prepares fabric for other finishing processes	Improves colour and handle	Permanent	Visible	
Whitens fabric or yarn	Slight damage to yarns or fabrics (can be serious if process not carefully controlled)	Permanent (except wool, which gradually yellows)	Visible	
Flattens yarns	Increases absorbency	Durable	Visible	Table-linen, some dress and upholstery fabrics
"Sets" fabric width, with warp and weft threads at right-angles to each other (fabric must be fed in straight)	Fabric can be fed into machine faster than it comes out. This squashes warp threads and removes "relaxation shrinkage"	Usually durable, but fabrics stretched a lot may shrink back during pressing or laundering	Invisible (except for tenter marks along the selvedges)	
Burns off fibre ends that stick out from surface		Durable, although more fibre ends can be brought to surface if fabric is rubbed	Nearly invisible	
Cuts pile to same height or removes fuzzy fibre ends from surface (similar to singeing)	"Sculptured" effect to pile fabrics: before shearing, parts of pile are pressed flat; after shearing, these parts are steamed or brushed to make them stand up again.	Pile fabrics, permanent; other fabrics, durable (see singeing)	Pile fabrics, visible; smooth fabrics, almost invisible	"Sculptured" carpets and velvet fabrics
Fibre ends are plucked out, forming fuzzy or hairy layer on surface. This can be cropped, or brushed to make nap lie in one direction	Tends to weaken fabric	Durable, but heavy wear can wear it off	Visible	Some fur fabrics; blankets; Viyella; flannel; flannelette; brushed nylon
Flat cotton fibres swell up and straighten out	Fabric or yarn becomes softer, stronger and more absorbent (which means it takes dye better)	Permanent	Visible	Cotton sewing threads; dress fabrics; furnishing fabrics

continued

Name of finish	Purpose	When done	Fibres used on	How it is done
Calendering	To create smoother, more lustrous surface	One of the last finishing processes	All fibres, especially cellulosic and man-made	Fabric is fed between metal rollers which may be: smooth or patterned; cold or heated; moving at the same speed or at different speeds Pressure from rollers squashes threads, making them pack closer together
Puckered finishes	To create crinkled surface	During weaving or after basic finishing	All (different techniques for different fibres)	(a) Printing patterns using chemicals or heat (b) Stretching some warp threads tighter than others during weaving (c) Weaving with pattern of long ''floating'' crepe yarns on back
Burnt-out finishes	To create decorative pattern by making parts of fabric transparent	After basic finishing	Mixtures	Special chemicals are printed on fabric
Filling	To make fabric seem smoother and firmer	After other finishing processes	Mainly cotton	Fabric soaked in starch before calendering
Performance finishes				
Flame-resistant	To make fabric less flammable	At yarn or fabric stage, after other finishing processes	Mainly cotton; also acrylics, viscose, nylon, polyester	Fabric saturated with special chemicals. Sometimes also treated with special resin.
Trubenising (trade name)	Stiffening	After other finishes or during making up	Cotton	Fabric treated with chemical which changes structure of fibres
Drip-dry finish	To remove need for ironing	After basic finishing	Cellulosics	Fabric treated with special resins which soak into fibres

Effect it has	Other effects	Durability	Visibility	Common uses/ Trade names
Fabrics are often soaked in starch, waxes or resin before being calendered. This makes fabric feel stiffer and look shinier.	If rollers turn at different speeds, they polish fabric as well. Heated rollers give even higher polish. Engraved rollers emboss a pattern of bumps and hollows.	Temporary. If fabric soaked with resin, durable. Permanent on thermoplastic fabrics, because heated rollers make yarns melt slightly.	Visible	Chintz; cire; embossed fabrics; moire; glazed cottons
(a) Parts of fabric shrink, making rest of fabric pucker up (b) When the fabric allowed to relax, stretched yarns shrink back to normal length, so unstretched yarns ripple (c) Crepe yarns shrink making front of fabric stand up in bubbles, like quilting		Permanent, but (a) and (b) can be damaged by ironing.	Visible	(a) plisse, crinkle-finish fabrics; (b) seersucker; (c) matelasse, pique (French words, both meaning "quilting")
One set of fibres is eaten away (burnt-out) by chemicals, making them transparent		Permanent	Visible	Dress fabrics; sheer curtain fabrics
Starch fills spaces between yarns, making fabric look very smooth and lustrous	Also adds stiffness	Temporary (removed at first washing)	Invisible, unless fabric rubbed (see page 24)	Dress fabrics; bed-linen
Either forms coating which cuts off oxygen supply which all flames need; or chemically changes fibres	Increases cost of fabric, changes feel (most treated fabrics feel harder)	Durable (if cleaning or washing instructions followed carefully)	Invisible	Trade name: Proban
Makes fibres, and therefore fabric, much stiffer		Permanent	Invisible	Mainly shirt collars and cuffs
The structure of fibres is changed	Fabric can be weakened: less abrasion resistance and tensile strength. Some ironing usually needed.	Permanent, if washing instructions followed carefully	Invisible	Shirts, blouses, dress fabrics.

continued

Name of finish	Purpose	When done	Fibres used on	How it is done
Durable press	To remove need for ironing	After other finishing processes	Cellulosics	(1) Fabric is saturated with special resin then dried in tenter machine (2) Garment is cut out, made up and pressed. (3) Finished garment is baked in special oven to 'cure' resin
Water repellent	To stop water soaking into fabric, but allow air to pass through	After basic finishes (and to finished articles)	All	The fabric is coated with special finish (usually silicone)
Waterproofing	To prevent any water passing through fabric	After other finishing processes (and to finished articles)	Mainly cotton	The fabric is completely covered with layer of wax, rubber, or resin
Stain repellent	To prevent dirt and grease clinging to fabric	After most other finishes (and to finished articles)	Most	Fabric is coated with special finish (containing silicone and fluorine)
Anti-static	To prevent fibres developing static electric charge (Static makes fabrics cling to one another, attracts dirt and dust; can cause sparks and mild electric shocks.)	During or after finishing (or during spinning of synthetic filaments).	Acetate and synthetics	Finish is added to surface of fibre
Non-shrink	To prevent relaxation shrinkage. Most fabrics are stretched lengthwise during knitting, weaving and finishing (see page 181). When washed or damp-pressed, they shrink back to their normal length. This is relaxation shrinkage.	After basic finishing	a) Cotton, linen, some rayons b) Wool	a) Fabric is fed into tentering machine faster than it will come out, or damp fabric is pressed against stretched blanket (or rubber sheet) and heated. Blanket then allowed to go back to normal size with fabric still in place. b) Fabric dampened and left to
Shrink-resist	To prevent shrinkage because of felting (see page 92)	Any stage from carding fibres to finished articles	Wool	(a) Wool is treated with chlorine or other chemicals, or (b) given a very thin coating of synthetic resin, or a combination of both
Mothproof	To protect from attack by larvae of clothes moth and carpet beetle	During dyeing	Mainly protein fibres	Chemicals are added to dye-bath

Effect it has	Other effects	Durability	Visibility	Common uses/ Trade names
Process changes the fibres	Making-up can be difficult (problems with stitching, pressing, alterations). Loss of strength: less abrasion resistance and tensile strength. Fabrics may feel stiffer.	Very durable, but care needed with washing and drying	Invisible	Mostly used for trousers and shirts. Trade names: Koratron, PP Super Crease, Sanforized Plus, Dan-Press, Coneprest.
Drops of water cannot spread out and soak in. Instead they stay round, and roll off	Works best on very closely-woven fabrics	Durable, care taken with washing and cleaning. Renewable. Finish can be damaged if article gets very dirty.	Invisible	Raincoats, anoraks, coats Trade-name: Scotchguard
Spaces between yarns are filled up, so there are no gaps for water to get through	Air and body moisture cannot pass through very clammy to wear. Tends to stiffen fabric	Permanent	Visible	Raincoats, oilskins, tents, tarpaulins
Grease and dirt cannot cling to fibres; very similar to water-repellency		Durable. Renewable.	Invisible	Carpets, velvets, upholstery, some clothing fabrics
Fibres become a little more absorbent. Water is a good conductor of electricity, so this helps get rid of static charge.		Durable, but repeated washing will weaken. Rinsing in solution of Stergene, or fabric softener helps reduce static.	Invisible	Carpets, clothing (especially lingerie) Trade-names for anti-static fibres: Ultron, Antron
Warp yarns return to their normal length		Permanent (although fabrics may shrink a little more in use)	Invisible	Fabrics for clothing and furnishing Trade-names: Sanforized, Rigmel
(a) Chemical eats away tips of scales on fibres, or (b) Resin fills spaces between scales and fibres.	Does not prevent relaxation shrinkage	Permanent	Invisible	Machine washable wool. Trade-name: Superwash
Changes fibres so larvae no longer like taste		Permanent	Invisible	Clothing and furnishing fabrics; carpets and rugs

Look again at picture 6, between pages 106 and 107. Can you tell which finishing processes listed in the table have been used to create the different fabrics?

Have you, or any of your friends or family, owned any textiles with special finishes? Were you pleased with them, or were you disappointed? Why do you think this was?

Try to collect examples of as many different finishes as you can. They may be scraps from the bit-box, or items of clothing or furnishings. If any of them still have labels attached, you may find some information about special finishes there. If not, try to work out for yourself how each fabric or yarn has been finished.

You can find out more about finishes by carrying out some of the following investigations. You could share your results, together with your collection of different textiles, by putting up a display somewhere in your school.

Cleaning and bleaching

Note: If you carry out this investigation with a large enough piece of loom-state fabric (about 50 cm square), you can cut samples from it for some of the later investigations.

Cut a 5 cm square from your sample, to remind you what it was like to start with.

Wash the rest of the sample thoroughly with soap and hot water (if you are using calico you may have to boil it, to get it really clean).

After rinsing, soak it in a 3% hydrogen peroxide solution for about 8 hours (or overnight). Rinse it thoroughly, smooth it out (do not iron it) and let it dry. Compare it with the original fabric. Apart from the colour, does the fabric look or feel different in any way?

Hydrogen peroxide is corrosive and you must be careful not to get it on your skin or in your eyes. Wear goggles when lifting the fabric into or out of the solution, and rubber gloves on your hands.

Tentering

Collect examples of selvedges from as many different types of fabric as possible. Look for marks made by a tentering machine.

Find out: how to "block" knitwear before making-up; how to stretch embroidery and canvas work. (Both these processes are really a small-scale version of tentering.)

Shearing

Do not try singeing – it is difficult to do properly and could be dangerous.

If you roll the sample of bleached fabric over your finger and hold it up to the light, you will be able to see the fibre ends sticking up.

With an electric razor, carefully shave a small (10 cm) area of the fabric. When you are sure that you have given it a really close shave, spread the fabric out flat and see whether it has changed the appearance of the fabric in any way.

Try shaving other fabrics, from cast-off clothing or furnishings, for example.

Napping

Try napping your own fabric: cut a small (10 cm) piece of bleached fabric and use a wire brush to fluff up the surface.

Compare it with the fabric it was cut from. How much difference have you made to the way it looks and feels? Try brushing several different fabrics, made from different fibres or types of yarns. Are some of them easier to brush than others?

Mercerising

In 1853 a fabric printer called James Mercer made an interesting discovery. He picked up a piece of cotton cloth that had been used to filter caustic soda (used in dyeing) and noticed that it looked softer, and more lustrous. He later discovered that it had become stronger and more absorbent as well.

Cut two 5 cm square pieces from your sample of bleached fabric. Staple one of the pieces to a thin piece of scrap wood (put the staples close together, round all four sides). Ask your teacher to soak both pieces of fabric in an 18–25% sodium hydroxide solution for about $1\frac{1}{2}$ minutes and then wash and dry the samples. (Leave the first sample stapled to the wood until it is dry.) Compare them with the rest of the fabric, and with each other. The soaking must be done by a teacher because sodium hydroxide is dangerously corrosive.

Calendering

Shear a piece of bleached fabric then "calender" it with an electric iron. Put a piece of stiff card under the fabric, and press quite hard with the iron as you slide it to and fro. Compare your calendered fabric with the piece that has only been sheared.

Find out how permanent your calendering is by cutting your sample in half and washing one of the pieces.

Puckered finishes

Take care not to burn yourself. Wear oven gloves or hold the wire in tongs.

Heat a piece of wire or a skewer in a gas flame or bunsen burner. Run it along a piece of thermoplastic fabric and notice what happens. When it has cooled, feel the fabric – you may find that the heat has made it feel quite different. This is because you used too much heat: in a textile factory they can control this much better than you can.

Weave a small piece of fabric, stretching one or two groups of warp threads really tight. Notice what happens when you take the finished sample off the loom or frame.

Simple flame-resistant treatment

Mix a solution of 7 parts by volume borax and 3 parts by volume boric acid. Cut 4 strips (5 cm × 12 cm) from the same piece of cotton fabric, and soak two of them in the borax solution.

Leave them to dry naturally, and then carry out a burning test (see page 175), using one piece of treated fabric, and one that has not been treated. How much more flame-resistant is the treated fabric?

Wash the two remaining pieces of fabric (one treated, one untreated). Let them dry naturally, and then repeat the burning test. Is this flame-resistant treatment permanent, durable, or temporary?

Water repellence

Collect 10 cm squares of different fabrics (e.g. denim, gabardine, dress cotton, tafetta).

Cover half of each sample with a piece of card or paper, and treat the rest of the sample with a water-repellent spray like Scotchguard. Read the instructions on the spray can carefully and follow them exactly.

Let the samples dry naturally, take the card off, then carry out a water-repellency test (see page 174).

Watch the samples carefully – is there any difference between the treated and the untreated parts of the sample? How successful is the treatment?

Repeat the experiment, but this time hang the samples up, when doing the water repellency test, instead of stretching them over a jam-jar. Spray them with water, and shake them gently, to imitate the way garments move when you are wearing them.

Stain repellence

Treat some 15 cm squares of fabric with a stain-repellent spray, covering one half of each sample as you did for the last investigation.

Collect different types of dirt and grease, and drop small amounts of each on the samples. Watch the samples for a few minutes, then give them a gentle shake and examine them again. How much difference is there between the treated and untreated areas?

Wash the samples in warm soapy water. Is there any difference between the treated and untreated areas now?

SEE ALSO

Dyeing and printing for information about another important finishing process–adding colour and pattern to textiles.
Safety for more about the flammability of fabrics and yarns.
Tests for help with designing more tests to compare different finishes.

See the book *Home and Consumer* (in this series) for information on stain removal.
Textile Science by Gohl and Vilensky (Longman).

Instructions

 Collect as many different types of instructions as you can, e.g. for equipment, games (board games, computer games), craft techniques, knitting patterns, sewing patterns, kits (crafts, self-assembly furniture).

Find out how good you are at following instructions by trying the exercise below. If you are doing this as a group, work in complete silence, as though it were an exam, and see who finishes first.

1 You will need a piece of plain writing paper, a ruler, a pencil and a pair of scissors.
2 Read through the instructions before you start work.
3 Write your name in the top right-hand corner of the paper.
4 Write the date in the bottom left-hand corner of the paper.
5 Rule a line down the middle of the paper.
6 Cut half-way up this line.
7 Fold the right-hand flap upwards, so that it covers your name. The edges of the paper should meet exactly. Crease well.
8 Take the top edge of this flap and bring it down to touch the fold. Crease well.
9 Fold the left-hand flap back, underneath the paper.
10 Fold the paper in half, so that the left-hand flap is facing you, and the fold is on the left.
11 Measure along the fold exactly 10 cm from the top of the paper and make a pencil mark on the fold.
12 Make a crease from this point up to the top right-hand corner of the paper.
13 Open out the paper and cut carefully along all the crease lines.
14 When you have written your name and the date, don't do any more. Sit and fiddle with your pencil and ruler until the rest of the group have finished.
15 If you no longer have one complete sheet of paper, count how many pieces you are left with.
16 Carefully pack away your scissors, pencil and ruler.

How many pieces of paper did you have at the end of this exercise? If you had more than one, it means you broke the first rule of instructions – **read all the instructions really carefully before you start doing anything**. It may take a little more time, but in the long run you will find it is well worth while.

Instructions are important, and the people who write them try to make them easy to follow. Sometimes they succeed, and sometimes they do not.

You may come across some instructions that are so badly written they are impossible to follow. If so, you would be doing yourself, and other people, a service if you wrote a polite letter to the manufacturer asking them to explain what they mean.

Here are some hints to help you make the best use of instructions:

● At each stage, make sure you are looking at your work from *exactly* the same position as the people who wrote the instructions (figure 72). That way you are less likely to get something back-to-front, upside-down or inside-out.

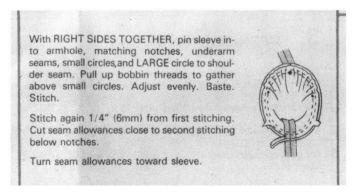

With RIGHT SIDES TOGETHER, pin sleeve into armhole, matching notches, underarm seams, small circles, and LARGE circle to shoulder seam. Pull up bobbin threads to gather above small circles. Adjust evenly. Baste. Stitch.

Stitch again 1/4" (6mm) from first stitching. Cut seam allowances close to second stitching below notches.

Turn seam allowances toward sleeve.

Figure 72
(a) *Part of dressmaking pattern instructions.*
(b) *Work laid out as in the instructions.*

• Always start by reading *all* the instructions right through. It will help you to understand how the different stages of the work "fit" together. If you come across something you do not understand, hunt around to see if it is explained in another part of the instructions.

• Sometimes instructions can be difficult to understand if you are making something that starts as many different pieces, like a textile jigsaw puzzle. A "dummy run" can often help at this stage: roughly fix the pieces together as you go through the instructions. You will have to take it all apart again, but at least you will understand what all the bits of the jigsaw are for.

• When you start work, concentrate on one stage at a time. Study the instructions for each stage carefully, before you begin to follow them. Do not be tempted to skip anything until you are a real expert (and even then, take care).

• If you still find one particular stage difficult to understand, read through the instructions for the next stage or two; again, knowing what comes next always helps.

• If you get really stuck, discuss the problem with a friend. If you still cannot work it out, ask your teacher for help – but try to imagine *you* were the teacher and how you would react to the different students in figure 73.

Figure 73

With a group of friends, look through your collection of instructions. You will probably find that some of them are easier to understand than others.

Sort them out into two groups: (1) those that look easy to follow, and (2) those that look particularly difficult.

What is it about each group that makes them look easy, or difficult? Would some diagrams (or better diagrams) have helped?

Could you re-write one of the examples in the second group to make it easier to understand?

Try your hand at writing instructions. Divide into small groups (2 or 3 in each group) and write instructions for one of these: a paper aeroplane, a very simple pencil-case, an embroidery stitch, twill weave on a weaving card, a macramé knot, skeining wool ready for dyeing, making a simple screen-print.

Give your set of instructions to someone who has not done it before (maybe a younger pupil in school), and see how they get on.

Knitted fabrics

Collect a large number of small fabric scraps; a magnifying glass or low-power microscope (×20); knitting needles (various sizes); some knitting yarns.

There are two main types of knitted fabric: weft knitted and warp knitted.

Weft knitting

In weft knitted fabrics, the yarn runs across the fabric, making loops with the row beneath (figure 74). It is called a weft knitted fabric because the yarn travels in the same direction as the weft yarns in weaving. If different coloured yarns were used for each row, a weft knitted fabric would have *horizontal* stripes.

Because of the loops, a weft knitted fabric will always stretch, no matter what it is made from. Pull it, and you can see how the loops change their shape.

Figure 75 shows some fabrics that can be made on weft knitting machines. The main types are listed here.

Figure 74 A simple weft knitted fabric.

a) **Jersey, or single jersey or plain knit**
Hand-knitters call this stocking-stitch (one row plain, one row purl). This is the basic fabric that a single-bed domestic knitting machine produces. It stretches more sideways than lengthways. It is often used for t-shirts.

b) **Rib knit or ribbing**
Both sides look the same, with the ribs of plain and purl running up the fabric. It is very elastic, stretches well sideways and snaps back into shape quickly. You may have a jacket that is made from a woven fabric, with ribbing used for the waistbands and cuffs.

c) **Purl knit**
Hand-knitters call it garter stitch (every row plain, or every row purl), and it is the first stitch that most of them learned to do. Both sides look the same. It stretches the same in both directions.

d) **Double jersey or double knit**
Made on a machine (called a ''double bed'') that uses two sets of needles, each with its own supply of yarn. Because it uses twice as much yarn it is thicker than single jersey, although a lot depends on the type of yarn it is made from. It makes a firm fabric that lies flat, and has much less stretch than single jersey.

e) **Interlock**

This is the name of a machine which makes fabric rather like a thin double-knit. It is used mainly for underwear (look at cotton pants and vests), but you may find some t-shirts and lightweight dresses made from it. Interlock is nearly always knitted in one colour, usually from fine cotton yarn, and often has patterns added by printing.

Figure 75 Weft knitted fabric samples.

Some facts about weft knitting

- If you knit by hand, or on a domestic knitting machine, you are making weft knitted fabric.

- Plain weft knitted fabrics (called "single jersey") tend to curl at the edges, which can make them difficult to work with.

- Weft knitting can be light-, medium- or heavy-weight, depending on the thickness of the yarn, and the size of the loops. (You may not see many very light-weight weft knits, because they do not keep their shape well enough to be really useful.)

- There are hundreds of different stitches in weft knitting. They are used to create textures, and also to change the fabric's properties (for example, thickness, elasticity, drape).

- If different coloured yarns are used, weft knitting can produce an enormous variety of patterns. These can be simple horizontal stripes, all-over patterns, pictures, or single motifs.

- Some weft knitting stitches can only be done by hand, some can only be done by machine, and some can be done by either.

- Weft knitted fabric can be made from man-made or natural fibres, and from filament or staple yarns.

- Weft knitting can make straight lengths of fabric, which is cut out and stitched up just like woven cloth (the "cut-and-sew" method).

- It can also make shaped fabric pieces that are ready to be stitched up. (Garments made like this are often called "fully fashioned".)

- It can make tubes of fabric (circular knitting), which is useful for tights and socks, where seams could be uncomfortable. You may find tubular fabric sold in shops, but it is usually cut, opened out and sold as flat fabric.

- Circular knitting machines are very popular in factories, because they are so economical to use: they are faster, and they take up less space than flat machines. (A circular machine 1 m in diameter can knit fabric that measures 3 m wide when opened out flat.)

- Most industrial knitting machines (and some domestic ones, as well) are now controlled by computers. Because of this, and because weft knitting machines are very quick to set up, it is easy to produce new patterns as soon as there is a change in fashion.

- Weft knitted fabrics will often "ladder" if they are cut, or if a thread is broken. This means that things made by the "cut-and-sew" method must be stitched together very carefully, to prevent the fabric laddering at the seams.

- Nobody knows exactly when hand-knitting began. Pieces of knitted fabrics dating back to AD 250 have been found.

- The first knitting machine was invented in 1589 by an English clergyman (Reverend William Lee).
- The circular knitting machine was invented about 200 years ago.

Figure 76 A simple warp knitted fabric.

Warp knitting

In warp knitted fabrics, the yarns run *up* the fabric, like the warp yarns in weaving (figure 76). If different coloured yarns were used, the fabric would have *vertical* stripes.

There are four types of warp knitting machine: Raschel, Tricot, Milanese, and Simplex. Between them, these four types of machine can create an amazing number of different fabrics. Figure 77 shows some samples of these.

Figure 77 Warp knitted fabric samples.

Some facts about warp knitting

- Warp knitting did not start as a hand-craft, like weft knitting and weaving. The first warp knitting machine (a Tricot machine) was invented in 1586. Warp knitting can still only be done by machines, in factories.
- It usually only makes fabric in flat sheets (like woven fabrics).

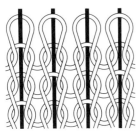

Figure 78 Stocking stitch with yarn woven into it. A warp insertion fabric.

• Warp knitting is the fastest way to make cloth: the latest machines can produce over 50 metres an hour.

• Before a machine can start knitting, each warp yarn must be threaded into it separately; a wide fabric may need over 1000 warp yarns, which could take a whole day to thread up.

This is the main reason why warp knitting is not used for "fashion" fabrics; it would be too expensive to keep re-threading the machines every time the fashions changed.

• Warp knitting can be firm, like a woven fabric, or elastic (though not so stretchy as some weft knits).

• It keeps its shape well, so it can be used to make very fine, lightweight fabrics.

• Most warp knits do not ladder, which means fewer problems when cutting out and stitching up. (Some very lightweight fabrics will split apart if a thread is broken. They are generally only used for cheap pockets or jacket linings.)

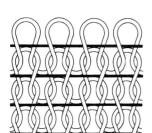

Figure 79 Diagram of simple weft insertion fabric.

Knit-weave fabrics

These fabrics are all made on knitting machines, but while they are being made, extra yarns are woven in. So they are called "knit-weave" fabrics.

Knit-weaves have some of the advantages of knitted fabrics (crease-resistant, lightweight, comfortable and cheap to make), and some of the advantages of woven fabrics (strong, and good at keeping their shape).

Figure 78 shows how you can make a knit-weave fabric yourself, by weaving an extra yarn in and out of a piece of hand-knitting. As you can see, the extra yarns go *upwards*, like the warp in a woven fabric, so this is called *warp insertion*.

If you pull your sample sideways you will find that it stretches like a knitted fabric; if you pull it lengthways it will behave more like a woven fabric.

When a machine makes this type of fabric, the weaving and the knitting are done at the same time.

Figure 79 shows a *weft insertion* fabric. This has extra yarns woven in *across the width* of the fabric. Which way do you think this fabric would stretch most?

Figure 80 shows how you can make a *warp and weft insertion* fabric. The warp yarns are woven into the knitting, just like in warp insertion. But if you look carefully, you will see that the weft yarns do not interlace with the knitting at all.

You may be able to make fabric with "laid-in" yarns like the one in figure 79 on your domestic knitting machine. (It is often called "weaving" in the instruction books.)

Figure 80 Diagram of a warp and weft insertion fabric.

Sew-knit fabrics

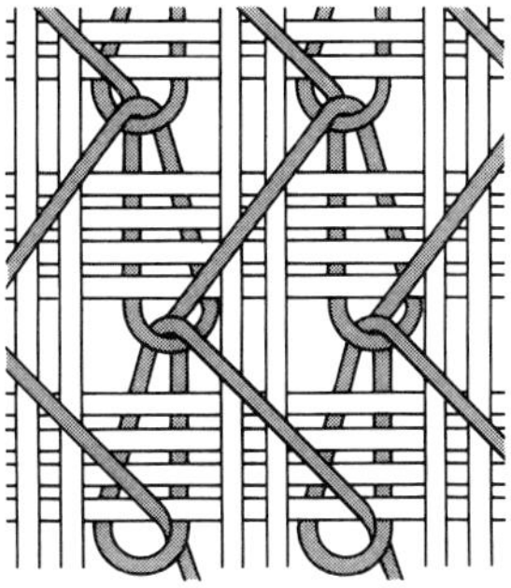

Sew-knit fabrics have a warp and weft, just like woven fabrics, but the yarns are not interlaced. Instead they are stitched together with a third yarn (figure 81), using either a stitch rather like warp knitting, or a chain-stitch (like the stitching done by a toy sewing machine). This makes them much quicker (and therefore cheaper) to produce than woven fabrics.

Malimo and Arachne are two of the best-known fabrics made in this way. They are not used much for clothing; you are more likely to find them used as furnishing fabrics.

Figure 81 Diagram of a simple sew-knit fabric.

How good are you at recognising knitted fabrics?
Hunt through your collection of fabric scraps and see how many knits you can find. You may need to examine them closely (use a lens or low-power microscope if you are not sure about some of them).

Sort through your clothes and the other textiles in your home. If you have a fabric shop nearby, look there as well. How many knitted fabrics can you find? How many of them are weft knits? How many are warp knits, knit-weave or sew-knit?

Are there some things that always seem to be made from knitted fabrics? If so, are they always made from the same type of knitted fabric? Why?

You can find out a lot about weft-knitted fabrics by making some small samples yourself, by hand or machine. It would save time if you did this with a group of friends, especially if someone needs to learn how to knit. Discussing your results may lead you to further investigations. (You may want to put the samples in your course-work folder, but if not you could use them to make a patchwork blanket.)

Here are some ideas to get you started.

1) **Does the size of the loops affect factors like stretch, stiffness or thickness?**
Find out by making stocking-stitch samples with the same yarn, but using different sized needles for each one (or if you are using a machine a different stitch size).

2) **Does knitting use more yarn than weaving? Which takes longer to do? Do the size of the loops or the spacing of the warp and weft yarns make much difference?**

Find out by knitting and weaving some squares of fabric, noting how long each one takes. Make sure that all the squares are the same size, and made from the same type of yarn. The only variables should be the size of the loops and the spacing of the weaving yarns.

Then unpick the squares and measure the yarn you have used. If you do not want to destroy the samples, you could weigh them instead. (You may need to borrow some very accurate scales from the science lab for this.)

3) Does weft knitted fabric always curl at the edges?

Look at the samples you have already made: do they curl at the edges? If so, do some curl more than others? If so, what caused the difference?

Make some samples using different stitches, like garter stitch, moss stitch, k.1, p.1 rib, and k.2, p.2 rib. (Look them up in a knitting book, or ask someone to teach you.)

4) How much difference does a stitch make to properties like elasticity, stiffness or thickness?

Begin by examining the samples you made for the last investigation. Find out more by making samples of more complicated stitches like twisted stocking-stitch, brioche rib, woven stitch (sometimes called linen stitch).

5) Why is it important to check your tension before doing any hand knitting?

With a group of friends, each knit a sample from the instructions in figure 82, using exactly the same yarns and the same size needles.

You will need:
2 balls of knitting yarn (1 ball of colour A, and 1 ball of colour B);
A pair of knitting needles.

When everyone has finished, measure the length and width of each sample, and display them on the wall with some notes about the results.

Figure 82 A knitting pattern.

key: o = colour A
   * = colour B
   K = knit
   P = purl

Row

Cast off.

```
oooooooooooooooo     15 –K.   15   A
oooooooooooooooo     14 –P.   15   A
*oooo**o**oooo*      13 –K.   1B   4A 2B 1A 2B 4A 1B
**ooo**o**ooo**      12 –P.   2B   3A 2B 1A 2B 3A 2B
***oo**o**oo***      11 –K.   3B   2A 2B 1A 2B 2A 3B
****o**o**o****      10 –P.   4B   1A 2B 1A 2B 1A 4B
*****o**o*****       9 –K.    7B   1A 7B
oooooooooooooooo     8 –P.    15A
*****o**o*****       7 –K.    7B   1A 7B
****o**o**o****      6 –P.    4B   1A 2B 1A 2B 1A 4B
***oo**o**oo***      5 –K.    3B   2A 2B 1A 2B 2A 3B
**ooo**o**ooo**      4 –P.    2B   3A 2B 1A 2B 3A 2B
*oooo**o**oooo*      3 –K.    1B   4A 2B 1A 2B 4A 1B
oooooooooooooooo     2 –P.    15A
oooooooooooooooo     1 –K.    15A
```

Cast on 15.

SEE ALSO

Fabric construction for basic information about other ways of making fabrics.

Knit One, Purl One, by F. Hinchcliffe (Victoria and Albert Museum).
Machine Knitting to Suit Your Mood, by Johanna Davis (Pelham Books).
Textiles: Properties and behaviour in clothing use, by Edward Miller (B. T. Batsford Ltd)
Textiles, by N Hollen, J Saddler and A L Langford (Collier Macmillan Publishing).
The Fabric Catalog, by Martin Hardingham (Pocket Books New York).
Spinning and Dyeing the Natural Way, by Ruth A Castino (Evans Bros Ltd, London).

KEY WORDS
Warp the set of threads that run from end to end of a woven fabric.
Weft the thread that runs from side to side of a woven fabric, interlacing with the warp threads.
Warp knitted made from a set of yarns that travel up the fabric (like the warp threads in a woven fabric).
Weft knitted made by hand or machine using a yarn that travels from side to side of the fabric (like the weft threads in a woven fabric).

Labels

 Collect labels from textiles, things made from textiles and equipment used for textiles. Look for them at home, at school and in the shops.

    If you can, bring the labels to school. If you cannot, make a careful copy of each label and bring that instead.

A quiz

Figure 83 Some labels in common use.

1 Do you know what each of the labels in figure 83 means?
2 Where would you expect to find them?
3 If you were going to buy one of these, what would you like to know about it? What advice or information do you think should be on the label: a garment; a steam iron; a length of fabric; a ball of yarn; a soft toy; a bottle of printing ink?

Labels on textiles must, by law, tell you about the fibre content (figures 84, 85, 86). Do all the labels in your collection obey this law? What other information or advice can you find on each of the labels? What will be helpful when you are deciding what, or how much to buy? What will be useful later, when you are using the item?

Figure 84 Label from a roll of fabric.

Figure 85 Label from a garment.

Figure 86 Label from a ball of yarn.

With a group of friends, sort your labels into two groups:
1 Permanent labels – that have been firmly fixed in place and are obviously meant to stay there for the life of the item.
2 Temporary labels – that are meant to be removed before the item is used.

Do any of the temporary labels contain information that would be important after you had bought the item? If you were the manufacturer, would you have put this information on a permanent label?

Why do you think this has not been done?

Discuss this problem with a group of friends. Perhaps you can think of a way of making sure that important information like this does not get lost.

Design labels for your own craft product: a swing-ticket, with your own brand-name or logo, and details like price and size; and a sewn-in label.

SEE ALSO

Choosing fabrics, Equipment, Rights and responsibilities for more information and ideas about what to look for when you are buying things.

The topic on *labelling* in the book *Home and Consumer* (in this series) for information on the International Textile Care Codes system of labelling items made from textiles.

Man-made fibres

Send for *Better Living with Man-made Fibres* from the British Man-made Fibres Federation (address on page 197).

Figure 87 The lengths of time we have been using different fibres.

For thousands of years people managed quite nicely with their four main fibres (figure 87). When they were cold they wore wool, or padded cotton. When they were hot they wore cotton or linen. When they wanted to look especially grand they wore silk.

linen	xxxxxxxxxxxxxxx x xxxxxxxxxxxxxx xx xxxxxxx xxxxx xxxxx xxxxxxxxxxxxxxxxxx
cotton	xxxxxxxx xxxxxxxxxxxxxxxxxxxxxxxxxxxxxxxxxxxxxxxxxxxxxx
silk	x xxx xxxxx xxxxxxxxxxxxxxxxxxxxxxxxx xxxxxxxxxxxxxxxxxx
wool	x xxxxxxxxxxxxxxxx x xxxx xxxxxxxxxxxxxxx xxxxx
man-made fibres	x

(x = 100 years)

But people have never been happy to leave things the way they are. Old things have to be improved, or new ones invented. Sometimes this is because they are really needed. Often it is just because the idea is interesting and challenging.

In 1664 a scientist called Dr Robert Hooke looked at some silk-worms making their cocoons and began to think "Surely it must be possible for people, who are so clever, to do what these little grubs are doing. After all, they are only squirting some liquid through little holes."

He was right, of course, but it took another 220 years of trial and error before someone (a French chemist, Count Hilaire de Chardonnet) finally managed it.

Figure 88 Spinneret in use in industry.

It was fairly easy to copy the silk-worm's way of extruding liquid through a spinneret. In fact, humans improved on it. The silk-worm can only make two filaments at a time but, by making their spinnerets with lots of holes (figure 88), scientists can make as many filaments as they like. Today there are spinnerets that can make over 12 000 filaments at once.

Because we can change the size or shape of the holes, we can also make the filaments thick or thin, or different shapes – something else that the silk-worm cannot do. And man-made filaments can be much longer than silk filaments. There is a limit to how much liquid a silk-worm can make, but there is no limit to the amount of man-made liquid. If necessary, man-made filaments could be made millions of kilometres long.

What took the time was inventing a liquid that would coagulate (become solid) and turn into a strong, flexible filament.

By the end of the 19th century imitating the silk-worm had become more than just an interesting scientific idea. Ordinary people were getting better educated and their standard of living was improving. They were able to take more pride and interest in their clothes. Magazines told them what rich, fashionable people wore and they wanted to look like that, too. But pure silk was still too expensive; what they needed was a cheap, artificial silk.

In 1890, at about the same time as Chardonnet exhibited his "artificial silk", another French scientist called Louis Despeissis discovered how to make a useful artificial fibre.

Despeissis and Chardonnet made their fibres from *cellulose*, which they got from either wood, or the left-over fluff on cotton seeds (see page 104). We do not know what made them try cellulose. Perhaps they were copying the silk-worm, which has to eat a lot of it (in the form of mulberry leaves) in order to make its silk.

Fibres made from cellulose that has been destroyed and then re-made are called *regenerated cellulosic fibres*.

Despeissis dissolved the cellulose in cuprammonium (cupra = copper; ammonium = ammonia) and it made a liquid that would turn into filaments. It was known either as *Pauly's silk* or as *cupro* and is still made today, although it is an expensive process. If you see fabric made from this fibre now it will be called by one of these names: cupro, Bemberg, Bemsilki, Cupioni, Cupracolor, Cuprama, Cupresa, Dureta, Matesa or Tusson.

Once this breakthrough had been made, new or improved fibres seemed to be invented every few years.

1905

All these cellulose fibres used to be called rayon. This was confusing, because they had different properties. So today each one is known by its own name and the term rayon is no longer used.

An English weaving firm, Samuel Courtauld & Co Ltd, began making fibres from cellulose. They called it *viscose artificial silk*, and it was the first mass-produced man-made fibre. It has similar properties to cupro, but it was given a different name because the cellulose was dissolved in a sulphuric acid mixture. This viscose process, (developed from Chardonnet's invention) was cheaper than cupro and soon became much more important. Viscose was the most successful man-made fibre until synthetic fibres were invented 60 years later.

You probably use things made from viscose. You may have heard of names like Rayonne, Viloft, Fibro or Durafil, but most of the yarns and fabrics made from viscose are simply labelled viscose or viscose rayon.

1921

A firm called British Celanese Ltd began making yet another cellulose fibre. This was called *cellulose acetate*.

You will still find acetate in fabric shops, and in some of the things you buy, but mainly for linings. You are not likely to find whole garments made from it.

All these new fibres were made as continuous filaments, just like cultivated silk, because the original aim was to produce a cheap imitation of silk. The fabrics made from them were very shiny and slippery.

1925 Then it occured to someone that if the filaments were chopped into *staple* lengths they could be used to make a softer, bulkier, less shiny fabric. Soon, the new fibres were being used instead of cotton and wool, as well as instead of silk.

Since then, scientists and manufacturers have carried on working, trying to improve the fibres they already have, and to invent new fibres.

1934 The first *synthetic* fibre was developed, in Germany. It never became popular for clothing, but you probably use quite a lot of it in your daily life. It is called polyvinyl chloride (PVC).

1935 The first really successful synthetic fibre was invented, by some scientists working for an American firm called Du Pont.

Synthetic fibres are made from chemicals. These chemicals come from raw materials (such as oil) that do not make fibres in nature.

It made very fine yarns that were stronger, more elastic and tougher than any other fibre. Garments made from it could be washed and drip-dried. It was also *thermoplastic* – by heating it to the right temperature, it could be "set" into permanent pleats.

They called it *nylon*. Figure 89 shows a nylon yarn close up.

1939 The Second World War broke out, and this amazing new fibre reached Britain in the shape of parachutes for the troops and stockings for their girl-friends.

Most of the nylon you use will be called either nylon or, more usually, *polyamide*. But many manufacturers have worked hard to develop improved types of polyamide fibres and these are sold under special names like: Antron, Cantrece, Enkalon, Qiana, Nylsuisse, Nylfrance, Perlon, Tactel.

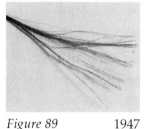

Figure 89
Nylon yarn.

1947 A Swiss firm found out how to make a different nylon yarn. It was textured and very elastic, and had an important effect on the clothes people wore. They called the new yarn *Helanca* (Figure 90).

Some other names for stretch nylon are: Agilon, Ban-lon, Fluflon, Saaba, Superloft, Synfoam, Textralized.

1950 Clothes appeared in the shops made from polyacrylonitrile fibres (*acrylics*, for short), and enjoyed huge success.

However, the first version of this new fibre turned out to have some disadvantages. So, manufacturers worked hard to improve things. Technological developments have now made acrylics one of the most desirable fibres for high-fashion knitwear.

Orlon, Acrilan, Courtelle, Dralon and Cashmilon are some of the best-known acrylic fibres.

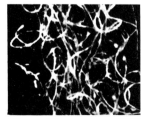

Figure 90
Helanca yarn.

1951 A new version of acrylic fibres was developed, called *modacrylic*. This had the great advantage of being flame resistant. The two best known modacrylic fibres are Dynel and Teklan. They are used where fire prevention is most important, in aircraft furnishings, soft toys and children's dressing gowns.

1953   *Polyester* fabrics arrived in the shops and once again everybody wanted them. They had all the advantages of nylon, but had a better "handle" and did not have the rather glassy shine of nylon.

Soon, manufacturers all over the world were making polyester in filament and staple form, and each one used a different name for it. You may have heard of names like Dacron, Diolen, Enkalon, Fortrel, Kodel, Lanon, Lavsan, Tergal, Terital, Terlenka, Terylene, Tesil, Tetoron, Trevira, Vycron.

1954   A new type of acetate was produced by the Celanese Corporation in America. It was called *cellulose triacetate* and is still popular today, because it is much cheaper than most of the synthetic fibres. You may have something in your wardrobe made from triacetate – it will probably be called Tricel, Courpleta or Arnel.

1955   In the mid 1950s three more new fibres were developed: *elastane, polynosic* and *chlorofibres*.

Elastane is a synthetic fibre, a variety of polyurethane. It is quite weak, but this does not matter because it is so elastic: a 3 cm piece of elastane filament will stretch to 1.5 m before it breaks.

Elastane filaments can also be very thin, much finer than the rubber which had been used for corsets since the early 1900s. For the first time, corsets, swimwear and other support garments could be really lightweight, comfortable and long-lasting.

In America, elastane fibres are known as spandex. You may also have heard them called Lycra, Vyrene or Blue C Elura.

Polynosic fibres are regenerated cellulose, like viscose, but with several advantages. They are much stronger, especially when wet, and are not so easily damaged by heat or chemicals. In fact, polynosic fibres have more of the properties of cotton than any other man-made fibre, except the hollow viscose fibres.

Modal and Vincel are other names for polynosic fibres.

Chlorofibres are synthetic fibres which have several important properties.

They are flame resistant, and cannot be damaged by sunlight, bleach, acids or alkalis. They are also the only fibres that generate negative static electricity when they are worn next to the skin. This seems to make underwear made from chlorofibres a great comfort to people who suffer from complaints like rheumatism. Other fibres generate positive static electricity, which is a nuisance – see page 112.

A blend of chlorofibre and Courtelle which has thermal insulation properties is sold under the brand-name Damart. Rhovyl, Saran, Velon and Vinyon are some of the trade names for chlorofibres.

1968 An American firm called Du Pont announced that they had made a new kind of nylon which they called *Qiana*. It was the nearest anyone had got to a really silk-like fibre, and was better than ordinary nylons and polyesters in many ways (crease-resistance, strength, much easier to dye and print).

1970s New fibres like the *polyolefins* (polypropylene and polyethylene) and *aramid* were developed. Although you are not likely to find polypropylene in any of your clothes, you have probably used it to tie up parcels, or walked on it (it makes very hard-wearing, stain-resistant carpets) or seen it advertised under the trade-names Meraklon or Ulstron.

Polyethylene is better known as polythene. Although it is not often made as a fibre, you may find it used in some of your clothes – it is one of the adhesives used on fusible (iron-on) interlinings.

Aramid is short for "aromatic polyamide". It is a variety of nylon with such special properties that it has been given its own generic name (see page 179). Aramid fibres are so exceptionally strong and flame-resistant that they are used in clothes for racing-car drivers, fighter pilots and space crews. This type of aramid fibre is known as Nomex. Another type (Kevlar) is used for bullet-proof jackets, protective clothing in factories and ropes which are many times stronger than steel.

Research into improving old fibres and developing new ones is still going on, but it is very different from what it was in the past. Scientists used to start by inventing or discovering a new fibre, and then had to find out what properties it had and what it could be used for. Now they start with a purpose and a list of properties, and design a fibre or a blend of several fibres to suit it. Figure 91 shows you how *you* might make a man-made fibre.

Talk to people who are old enough to remember when some of today's man-made fibres were new. Ask your parents and grandparents. Perhaps your teacher could arrange for you to visit an old people's home and talk to the men and women who live there; some of them may even remember the early days of artificial silk.

Ask them what it was like when each of the new fibres came into the shops. Did it make a difference to the sort of clothes they wore? Did it make life easier? Did it change the way they brought up their children, or the clothes they chose for them? Did they have any disasters, because they did not know how to care for things made from new fibres?

RECIPE FOR A MAN·MADE FIBRE

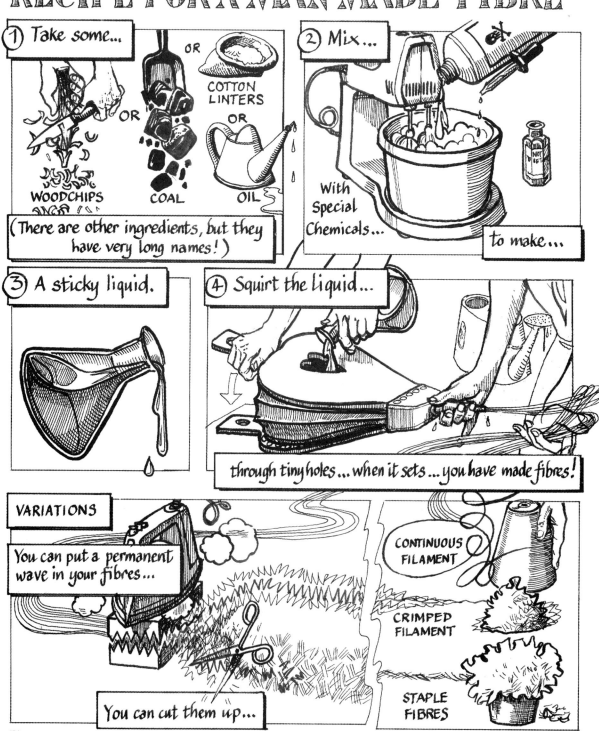

Figure 91

Ask them about the Second World War – about the first nylon stockings, and second-hand parachutes.

Ask them how they managed before permanent pleating, drip-dry fabrics or iron-on interlinings.

Figure 92 Pie-chart showing proportion of world use of natural and man-made fibres.

Do you know how many man-made and natural fibres you use?

KEY

☐ Cotton

▤ Wool

▨ Regenerated cellulosics

☐ Synthetics

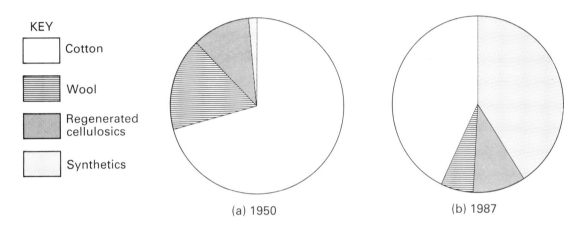

(a) 1950   (b) 1987

Find out by going on a Fibre Hunt.

Look at the labels in the clothes you and your friends are wearing. What are they made from? Look at the labels on all the other textiles you use – carpets, sheets, curtains, tents, fishing lines, crash-helmets, as well as clothes.

Then look also at items not made from fabrics. Look in mail-order catalogues, reference books, copies of *Textiles*, and visit different places: sports shops, hardware shops, builders' merchants, motor-bike specialists and as many more as you can think of.

Present your findings visually. Filling in a chart like Figure 93 is one possible way of doing this. Fill in one space on the chart for each item you find made of each fibre.

WOOL							
COTTON							
LINEN							
SILK							
POLYAMIDE							
POLYESTER							
ACRYLIC							
ACETATE							
VISCOSE							
TRIACETATE							

Figure 93

Which fibres seem to be used most? Why do you think this is? Which seems to have the most *different* uses? Which fibres are used least? Why do you think they are used so little? What are they used for?

What are all these fibres (man-made and natural) really like to use and to look after?

You know a lot about this already, because you use so many of them in your daily life. You know even more about them if you do your own washing and ironing. With a group of friends, discuss the fibres you use. Are there some that you really like or dislike? What is it about them that makes you feel that way?

Have any of you had clothes or household textiles spoiled because they were washed or ironed the wrong way? If so, make a note of what they were made from and what happened to them.

Do you, your family or friends have any things made from fibres that have worn out or been damaged sooner than you had expected? Make a class collection of these items and see if, between you, you can work out why the damage happened.

What advice would you give to the owners of these things, to help them avoid making the same mistakes again?

SEE ALSO

Fibres, for information about staple and filament fibres.
Fibres from plants, for relevant details about silk.
Properties of fibres chart.

Mistakes

I was in a hurry...

I just glanced up for a moment...

I was getting tired...

My friend was telling me about...

I forgot to check...

... and then the machine jammed.

The annoying thing about most mistakes is that, looking back, we know that they need not have happened.

Nobody likes making mistakes – they always slow you up, they often cost you money, and they can sometimes make you feel very silly. But although they are annoying at the time, mistakes *can* be useful, if they teach you something. There is a lot of truth in the saying "Everybody makes mistakes, but only a fool makes the same mistake twice".

So when you make a mistake, try not to get too upset about it – this is a time when you must be able to think clearly. If necessary, put the work away for a while and come back to it when you feel calmer.

Start by working out why the mistake happened. Make up your mind not to do it again and then decide what to do about it.

Can you undo the mistake?
Can you do this without leaving any trace?
How long will it take?

If you cannot undo the mistake
Can you cover it up in some way?
Can you change your design to turn it into something good?

If you think you can do something about it, you will still need to **decide whether it will be worth the trouble**.
Think about the time involved: would it be quicker to scrap the work and start again from scratch?
Think about the cost: can you afford to buy a whole new set of materials?
Think about the quality of the finished item: if you decide to unpick the mistake, or cover it up in some way, will the finished result be good enough?

As you gain experience, you will not stop making mistakes (nobody ever does) – you just will not make them so often. And you will get better at making decisions like the ones above. You will find that, although mistakes can be very upsetting, you can usually do something about them, as long as you keep your head.

Figures 94–97 show some examples of mistakes. Discuss what you would do with these items if you were making them.

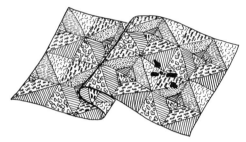

Figure 95 This patchwork was nearly finished when someone splashed coffee on it.

Figure 94 The top stitching round the edge of this bag has gone crooked in places. The stitches are so small they cannot be unpicked without damaging the bag.

Figure 96 The machine jammed and ruined a buttonhole on the front of this fine lawn blouse.

Figure 97 The knitting came off the machine and a whole row of stitches had to be put back on the needles. Unfortunately, not all the stitches went back on the right needles.

Mixtures and blends

Collect either two different types of fibre (e.g. nylon and wool) or two differently coloured fibres.

Figure 98 Label on a fabric made from a mixture of two different fibres.

When you go on your Fibre Hunt (page 139) you will probably find a lot of labels like figure 98, which have more than one fibre on them.

You can work out why two or more fibres are mixed together if you look at the *Properties of fibres* chart on page 148.

Imagine you needed a fabric that would be very strong, quick-drying, crease resistant and comfortable to wear. Look at the chart, and you will find that *nylon* has the first three properties. But if you look at nylon's other properties you will find that it is not absorbent and it is a poor conductor of heat, so it will not be that comfortable to wear.

Look for a fabric that is very absorbent and a good conductor of heat, and you will find that *cotton* scores very well. But on the other hand, cotton does not dry quickly enough, and it is not crease resistant.

The answer to your problem would be a fabric that had some of the properties of nylon, mixed with some of the properties of cotton. That way, the advantages of one fibre would help to cancel out the disadvantages of the other.

Look again at figure 98. Why do you think these fibres have been used together? (Your own experience of fibres and the *Properties of fibres* chart on page 148 will help you.)

How many other mixtures can you find? Look carefully through mail-order catalogues, and in various shops. What advantages do you think these mixtures have?

Mixtures, blends and bi-component fibres

What is the difference between a mixture, a blend and a bi-component fibre?

Blending happens *before* the fibres have been made into yarn. Two or more types of fibre are mixed together.

(a) Extrusion of side-by-side bi-component fibre

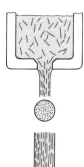

(b) Extrusion of core-and-sheath bi-component fibre

(c) Extrusion of bi-constituent fibre

Figure 99 Diagram of the production of three types of bi-component fibres, showing what each would look like if cut in half crossways and lengthways.

Take a bunch of each of two different fibres (or two differently coloured fibres). Put them together, then tease them out until they are thoroughly mixed. Twist the mixture into a yarn. This is a blended yarn.

Mixing happens *after* the fibres have been made into yarn. When fabric is being woven, two different yarns are used, each made from a different fibre or blend of fibres.

Weave a small piece of mixture fabric on a weaving card, as follows: use a bought yarn for the warp; use the blended yarn you made in the last activity for the weft.

Blends and mixtures can be made from any sort of fibre.

A **bi-component fibre** is made from a man-made fibre, before it coagulates (see page 134). Instead of just one type of liquid, two are used, and they are both squirted through the spinneret (extruded) at the same time. Figure 99 shows three different ways in which this is done.

Side-by-side bi-component fibres (figure 99(a)) are one way of giving a fibre a permanent crimp. They are usually made from two slightly different acrylics, or two slightly different nylons. Cantrece is a bi-component nylon; Orlon Sayelle is an acrylic bi-component fibre.

Core-and-sheath bi-component fibres (figure 99(b)) are useful for making melded fabrics (see page 146). A fibre that melts easily is chosen for the outer layer (the sheath).

Another way of making bi-component fibres is to mix the liquids together before they are squirted through the spinneret. Fibres made in this way are called **bi-constituent fibres** (figure 99(c)), and may be the next big break-through in man-made fibres.

SEE ALSO

Dyeing and printing for information about how fibres are coloured.
Fabric construction to see how yarns are made into fabric.
Man-made fibres.
Properties of fibres chart.
Yarns to see how blended fibres can be made into yarns.

"Non-woven" fabrics

Collect as many different types of fabric as possible.
    Collect some raw fleece or other animal fibres; samples of Vilene; terylene wadding; Bondaweb; felt; a J-cloth.
    A low-power (× 40) microscope or hand lens.
    Send for information packs from Vilene (address on page 200).

The costs of the different stages of making a fabric from its fibres might be:

	£			£
1 Fibres	w		1 Fibres	w
2 Spinning	x		..............o	
3 Weaving/knitting	y		..............o	
4 Finishing	z		2 Finishing	z
Total	£w + x + y + z		Total	£w + z

As you can see, it is much cheaper to make fabrics if the middle two stages are left out.

When fibres have been teased apart, ready for spinning, they look (from a distance, at least) rather like a sheet of fabric. But a fibre web like this would soon fall apart in your hands: if the web is going to be of any use as a fabric, something must be done to hold the fibres together. Until the 1950s this could only be done with animal fibres, which will *felt* together if they are soaked in hot water and then banged, rubbed and squeezed (see page 92).

You can make some felt yourself, if you have some raw fleece. First wash the fleece in hot water. Then, while it is still wet, spread it out and beat it with a block of wood. You will see it gradually shrink and mat together. (The felt for embroidered Numdah rugs from India is made this way.)

Today, improved technology and the development of synthetic fibres mean that almost any fibres can be used to make "non-woven" fabrics. Figure 101 shows how you might do this.

Figure 100 Close up of a fibre web.

Look through your collection of fabrics and see if any of them were made from fibre webs. Examine them closely with your lens or microscope. Can you work out how they were made?

MAKING NON-WOVEN FABRICS

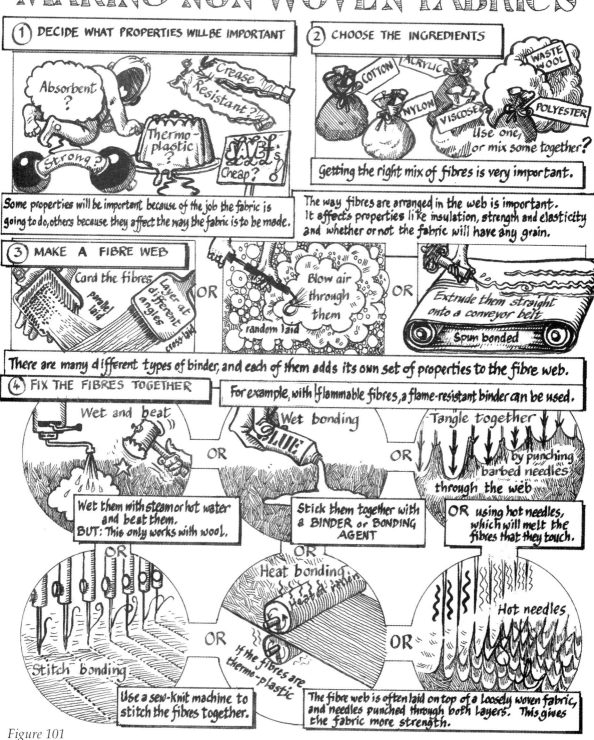

① DECIDE WHAT PROPERTIES WILL BE IMPORTANT

Absorbent?

Crease Resistant??

Thermo-plastic?

Strong?

SAVE £'s Cheap?

Some properties will be important because of the job the fabric is going to do, others because they affect the way the fabric is to be made.

② CHOOSE THE INGREDIENTS

COTTON
ACRYLIC
NYLON
VISCOSE
WASTE WOOL
POLYESTER

Use one, or mix some together?

Getting the right mix of fibres is very important.

The way fibres are arranged in the web is important. It affects properties like insulation, strength and elasticity and whether or not the fabric will have any grain.

③ MAKE A FIBRE WEB

Card the fibres.

parallel laid
Layer at different angles
cross-laid

OR

Blow air through them

random laid

OR

Extrude them straight onto a conveyor belt

Spun bonded

There are many different types of binder, and each of them adds its own set of properties to the fibre web.

④ FIX THE FIBRES TOGETHER

For example, with flammable fibres, a flame-resistant binder can be used.

Wet and beat

OR

Wet bonding
GLUE

OR

Tangle together

by punching barbed needles through the web

Wet them with steam or hot water and beat them. BUT: This only works with wool.

Stick them together with a BINDER or BONDING AGENT

OR using hot needles, which will melt the fibres that they touch.

OR

Stitch bonding

OR

Heat bonding
Heated roller
if the fibres are thermo-plastic

OR

Hot needles

Use a sew-knit machine to stitch the fibres together.

The fibre web is often laid on top of a loosely woven fabric, and needles punched through both layers. This gives the fabric more strength.

Figure 101

Compare different types of "non-woven" fabrics: crush them in your hand, then let go; pull them, in several different directions; hold them up by one corner and see how they drape; scratch the cut edges with your fingernail or a pin.

Do the same with knitted and woven fabrics that are roughly the same weight and thickness as the "non-woven" ones. What differences do you notice?

Visit some shops and look for "non-woven" fabrics. How many can you find? What are they used for?

Look at labels. What fibres are these fabrics made from? Find out if any of them need special care – in making up, in use or when being cleaned or laundered.

Compare the price of "non-wovens" with similar woven or knitted fabrics. Do you think they are good value for money?

Compare "non-woven" fabrics with true felt: test them for shrinkage, strength, abrasion-resistance and any other properties that might be interesting (see pages 169–75).

Be careful not to scald yourself.

Experiment with some true felt. Can you use any of its properties to create interesting textures? Here are some ideas to start you off: drip boiling water on it; wet it, or hold it over a steaming kettle, and then stretch it over a small ball or block of wood until it dries; brush it; quilt several layers together.

Try doing the same things to other "non-woven" fabrics.

SEE ALSO

Fibres from animals, for information about wool.
Man-made fibres, and *Properties of fibres* chart, for more information about the manufacture and properties of different fibres.

Properties of fibres

The more blobs the better	Abrasion resistance	Absorbency	Elasticity	Flame resistance	Insulation	Mothproof	Mildew resistance	Resistance to acids [1]	Resistance to alkalis [2]	Resistance to damage by bleach	Resistance to damage by sunlight	Static electricity	Tensile strength	Thermal conductivity [3]	Thermoplasticity [4]
COTTON	●●	●●●	●	●	●	●●●●	●	●●	●●●●	●●●	●●●	●●●●	●●●*	●●●	—
LINEN	●●●	●●●	●	●	●	●●●●	●	●●	●●●	●●●	●●●	●●●●	●●●*	●●●●	—
WOOL	●●	●●●●	●●●●	●●●●	●●●●	●	●	●●●	●●	●	●	●●●●	●	●	—
SILK	●●	●●●●	●●	●●●●	●●●	●●	●	●	●	●	●	●●●●	●●●●**	●	—
ACETATE	●	●●	●●	●	●●	●●●●	●●●●	●●●	●	●	●●●	●	●**	●	●●
ACRYLIC	●●●	●	●●●	●	●●●	●●●●	●●●●	●●●●	●●●	●●	●●●●	●	●●**	●	●●
POLYAMIDE	●●●●●	●	●●●●	●●	●●●	●●●●	●●●●	●		●●●	●●●	●	●●●●	●	●●●
POLYESTER	●●●●	●	●●●●	●●	●●●	●●●●	●●●●	●●●●	●●●●	●●●●	●●●●	●	●●●●	●	●●●●
TRIACETATE	●	●●	●●●	●	●●	●●●●	●●●●	●●	●●●	●	●●	●	●	●	●●●
VISCOSE	●	●●●●	●●	●	●●	●●●●	●	●●	●●●	●	●	●●●●	●●**	●●	—

1 Vinegar, some fruit juices, and perspiration are all mild acids.
2 Many washing powders are alkaline.
3 Means materials which are conductors of heat – they let body heat pass through them.
4 Means can be heat-set.

* = stronger when wet
** = weaker when wet

N.B. The way a fibre has been made into yarn, or the yarn into fabric,
can affect the properties of the fabric.
This list is, therefore, only a very general guide to properties.

On page 21 you were asked to make lists of the properties the fabrics in figure 14 should have, and to collect some more pictures of fabrics at work. What fibre or fibres do you think each fabric should be made from? What would be your second choice?

Research and investigation

Imagine you have been asked to design the costumes for a school production of *The Mikado*. All you know is that this is a comic opera about the Emperor of Japan, and that most of the characters are members of his Court.

The first thing you will need to do, therefore, is to make yourself a list of questions about Japanese costume, for example:

What were the shapes, fabrics and patterns like?

Was there a great difference between what the rich and the poor wore?

How did people like the Emperor show how important they were?

Will you be able to make yours in the same way, or will you have to adapt and simplify it?

Was there any difference between the men's and the women's clothes?

How much fabric did a garment take?

How did they cut and join the fabric?

Then think about where you might get the information:
reference books on Japanese history;
information from the Japanese Embassy in London;
museums and art galleries;
Japanese people, if there are any living near you.

Once you have gathered the information, you need to think about resources: time, people, equipment, materials, money.

You decide that your main problem will be making very cheap fabric look really rich and exotic under the stage lights. This must not take too long, or need too much special equipment. It must be something that your helpers can do without too much trouble.

How will you find out how to do this? You could:
● look for ideas in books on stage costume;
● get in touch with amateur or professional theatre companies to see if they can give you any tips;
● try out ideas on different types of cloth, to find out what works best under the stage lights;

- ask some of your helpers to try them out, to find which are easiest to do;
- work out the cost of each method.

Then you can decide which one works best and fits your budget.

The above is an example of how you might go about doing the research needed for a big project.

Whether you are buying, designing, making or arguing about something, you will always need knowledge. It will help you to make the best choices and be able to give reasons for your ideas. You may already have some of this knowledge. The rest you will have to find out for yourself.

Decide what you need to find out

Here are some examples, with a list of questions for you to discuss and add to.

a) **The study of a particular craft or technique**
When did it start? How was it done? What was it used for? What equipment was used? How is it done now? Could it be done any differently?

b) **Weddings**
What are the traditional wedding colours in this and other countries? Why? What sort of clothes do people wear for weddings these days? Are they different from other fashions? Has this always been so?

c) **Designing a play-tent for a child**
How big is the child? How many children will play in the tent? Where will the tent be used? Where should the openings be? Should it be decorated? If so, how? Will it need reinforcing anywhere?

You may not need to find answers to all your questions right at the beginning. Sort out what you need to know now, and what can be or may have to be left until later.

Whenever you can, discuss your work with some friends. They may ask questions you had not thought of. You may also find that, while you are working, more questions will occur to you.

Sort out what you know already

Note down any facts that you think might be useful. For example

a) Perhaps you know that the craft is practised in this country and in Africa (but you are not sure about other countries). If people practise the craft at your school, you will already have some idea about modern methods.

b) Think about weddings you have seen or been to. Have you seen any programmes about weddings in other countries on television?

c) If you know the child and his or her family, you will have some idea of how and where the tent will be used. You will also be able to guess whether it will be taken down each evening or left out overnight.

How will you find out the rest?

Research

Try looking up the information in books in your school library and local public library. The librarians will be only too happy to help you with your research. If they have not got what you need in stock, they can usually get it for you from another branch. If there is a college nearby, ask if you can visit their library to read and make notes.
(If you are researching something to do with people in the past, these is a lot of interesting material in books written at the time – your English teacher will probably be able to suggest some titles.)

Magazines and newspapers are also very useful. Newspaper publishers keep copies of every edition they have printed – some of them go back for hundreds of years. National and local newspapers will often let you use their store of back-numbers for your research, if you make an appointment.

The cartoons in old copies of *Punch* are very useful for information about what people thought and wore since 1852. Most public libraries keep bound volumes of *Which?* magazine, which are useful if you want to look up reports in back-numbers.

There are hundreds of "specialist" magazines that you never see on newsagents' shelves. Your newsagent will be able to tell you what is available, and can order copies for you.

Would **visits** to some of the following help in your research?
Shops: to find out what people are buying today, and to get ideas by examining ready-made items.
Art galleries and exhibitions: to see examples of the best textile crafts, past and present. Look at old portraits to see what rich people wore, the fabrics their clothes and furnishings were made from, and the embroidery that was used to decorate them.

Look at scenes with groups of people if you also want to see what ordinary people looked like. Study the backgrounds, to find out what homes were like.
Museums: to look at sculpture, collections of clothes, textiles, crafts, tools and equipment, from various countries. If possible, make an appointment to talk to one of the Curators or Keepers in the museum.
Factories and craftspeople: again, ring up or write to make an appointment.

Art school shows: to get ideas for textile crafts and fashion.

You could also **write** to

Foreign embassies: for information about the history, customs, crafts and clothes of the country.
Museums that are too far away to visit: for the answers to particular questions.

A note about writing letters
You are a busy person. If you found both letters in figure 102 waiting for you when you got home today, which one would you prefer to answer?

Figure 102

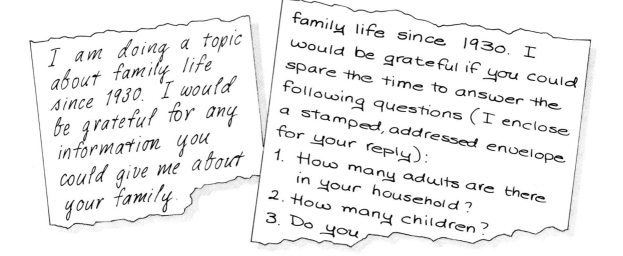

The people you write to are busy, too. They have not got time to write an essay for you.
1 Write clearly.
2 Give a short description of your topic, and what you have found out so far.
3 Ask questions that can be answered quickly. (If you can, do this on a separate sheet of paper, with spaces for the answers.)
4 Send a stamped addressed envelope for the reply.

You could **talk** to experts, older people, younger people: for information, ideas and different opinions.

Be quite clear in your mind what you want to find out when you are talking to people. It often helps to write out a list of questions first. Make notes on the spot. You may find it helps to use a tape-recorder.

If you are collecting facts and figures, a carefully worked out survey form is a great help. It means that you can note the answers quickly, and leave sorting out the information until you are back at school.

Investigations

Tests will help you to compare methods, materials or equipment. Before you carry out a test, be absolutely clear in your mind what you want to find out. (You will find some advice about designing fair tests on page 169.)

Experiments will help you find out what a material, a technique or a piece of equipment can do for you.

If you have carried out your research and investigations carefully enough, you will enjoy telling people about your work.

When someone (an examiner, perhaps) asks why you did something in a certain way, you can show them the results of your investigations and explain exactly why you made that decision.

If you make statements like "these days most men's underwear is still made from cotton" or "fashion changes when you are over 20", you will have the facts and figures to prove your point.

If you are asked "Will it stand up to the wear?" you will be able to describe the tests you carried out, and show people the results.

SEE ALSO

Design, Design sheets, Exams for ideas and information about research and investigations, and how to present your work.
Tests, for how to carry out some tests on fabrics.

Rights and responsibilities

As a consumer of textiles you have many rights, and these increase year by year. While you are reading this book, the Government is probably designing more regulations to protect you against dishonest or careless traders. Traders who do not obey these rules can get into very serious trouble.

- You are protected against some dangerous products or services by the **Consumer Safety Act** (1978).

   Children's nightdresses, anoraks and toys are covered under this Act. So is electrical equipment like irons, washing machines and sewing machines.

- You are protected against traders who might try to give you "short measure" by the **Weights and Measures Act**.

   If you pay for a 50 g skein of yarn, that is exactly what you should get. A 1 litre bottle of printing ink must contain exactly that amount. If you ask for 2.5 m of fabric, and the trader only gives you 2.25 m, he or she is breaking the law.

- You are protected against traders who do not tell the truth about a product or service by the **Trades Descriptions Act**.

   Textiles (and that means things made from textiles, as well) must have a label saying what they are made from, and this information must be correct. So must any other information that traders give you.

> If you are sold goods that don't match their description, or are not fit for their purpose, or are not of merchantable quality, you are entitled to have your money back.

> 91cm wide

> Crease-resistant finish

> Made in England

> Hand-spun

> Real leather

> Half recommended price

- You are protected against people selling you goods which are unfit for the purpose they are sold for by the **Sale of Goods Act**.

   If you buy a sweater, and the first time you put it on a stitch runs like in figure 103 the sweater is not "of merchantable quality".

   If you buy a screen-printing frame and the wood warps after you have used it a few times, it is not "fit for its purpose".

As a textile consumer you also have *responsibilities*. By keeping yourself informed, and refusing to put up with poor quality goods or services, you can help to make manufacturers and retailers improve their standards.

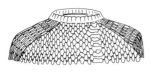

Figure 103

Make sure you know your rights.

Before buying anything, check that the label gives enough information about the product.

Examine goods thoroughly before you buy them.

Never let anyone persuade you to buy something you're not completely happy about. You are responsible for making the final decision.

If you don't really want to complain, but you think the product could be improved in some way, let the manufacturers know.

● Keep up-to-date with the laws and regulations about textiles and textile equipment.

● If you think you know of any goods or services that break any of these laws, tell the Trading Standards Officer at your local Town Hall or County Council Offices.

● If the label is breaking the law (by not stating what a textile is made from), do not buy the item, and politely tell the retailer why not.

● Check whenever possible that the information you are given is correct. For example, if you think a fabric looks wider or narrower than the label says, ask the retailer to measure it for you.

● Check the quality of the materials and the workmanship. Compare them with similar goods on sale elsewhere. If you think the item is poor value for money, do not buy it.

● If something goes wrong because you have used an item in a way it was not designed to be used, you won't get any compensation.

Be clear in your own mind about what you want an item for. Explain this to the retailer, and ask him or her to help you choose something suitable.

● Find out if *Which?* have recently tested the item you want to buy; if they have, study the report on the tests.

Find out if there is a British Standard for that type of item; if so, does the item meet that Standard?

Whenever you can, get advice from experts.

● Always get and keep a receipt for any goods or services you pay for. If you have to make a complaint it is useful to have proof of what (and when) you paid.

● It is the retailer, not the manufacturer, who is responsible to you if something goes wrong. If you are not satisfied with something you have bought, don't just grumble about it. Complain, politely but firmly, to the person who sold it to you, and ask for some compensation.

● If the shopkeeper refuses to give you any compensation, ask your local Consumer Advice Centre or Citizens' Advice Bureau for help and advice.

● Manufacturers, retailers and people who supply services are all keen to give the public what it wants. Complaints, suggestions and wise shopping habits are all ways in which you can help.

Get to know your local Citizens' Advice Bureau, Consumer Advice Centre and Trading Standards Office. Look in the telephone directory to find where they are. Visit them to meet the people who work there and find out more about what they do (telephone or write first, to find out the best time).

You could do this in groups, each of which could visit a different place and then report back to the rest of the class.

Carry out a survey (in school, or in your neighbourhood) into people's attitudes to these consumer organisations.
How many people know about them?
How did they learn about them?
If they have a problem, will they go to one of the organisations for help?
If not, why not? (The organisations might find the answers to this interesting.)
How will they decide which one to visit?

Is there a consumer group in your area? If there is, find out what they do, and decide whether you would like to join. If there is not one in your area, perhaps you would like to start one in school; the National Federation of Consumer Groups (address on page 200) will give you advice and help.

What advice would you give to someone in the situation in figure 104?

Figure 104

What would you do in this situation?

A family clubbed together to buy their granny her first electric sewing machine. She used the machine to make herself new curtains for her dining room, then began making some for her bedroom. Halfway through the second curtain, the machine started to smell of burning rubber and then topped dead.

The family takes the machine back to the shop, but the shopkeeper refuses to accept any blame because he says granny misused the machine: she had kept the bobbin winder in the "on" position all the time, which over-strained the motor. Granny says this is true, but she did not know it was important – there was nothing in the instruction book, and the shopkeeper had not said anything about it when he demonstrated the machine.

> Spacematic Electronic knitting machine for sale. All attachments. Barely used. Cost £565, will accept £150.

This looks like a bargain. It probably is, but it is a private sale. The machine may have been stolen, or be subject to a hire-purchase agreement. It may be faulty.

What are your rights if you have a problem with something you have bought from a private seller?

SEE ALSO

Equipment, for help with choosing textile equipment.
Labels, for more about what labels can tell you.
Shopping, for more about buying things.

For more about consumer information and protection see the book *Home and Consumer* (in this series).

(All addresses are on pages 197–200.)
A Handbook of Consumer Law published by Consumers' Association.
Reports on consumer matters from the National Consumer Council. (Send stamped addressed envelope for a list of titles. These reports are not free.)
Information about standards for textiles, things made from textiles, and equipment from the British Standards Institution.
Leaflets on household products and information about problems from Good Housekeeping Institute.
Consumer Rights Handbook by Anne Stansby, Pluto press, 1986.
Consumers: Know Your Rights by John Harries, Oyez-Longman.
How to Complain by Brigid Avison (Longman Self-help Guides), 1986.
How Not to Get Ripped Off by Barbara Lantin, Unwin, 1987.

Safety

Send for *Safety in Practical Studies* published by the Department of Education and Science; 1981 available from HMSO (address on page 198).
Material from your local Trading Standards Office, such as *Electricity and You – Safety*, *Electricity and You – Plugs and Fuses*.

Child blinded by sewing needle

FACTORY WORKER LOSES HAND

Batik accident puts school's star forward out of action

Foam-filled furniture kills again

Figure 105

Luckily textiles is an area where there are relatively few accidents, but that is not much comfort if you are the person who has been hurt or injured. When accidents happen, it is nearly always because someone has been careless – textiles has such a "safe" image that it is tempting to take safety for granted.

Safe equipment

All the equipment you use in school is safe. Your teachers will have chosen makes and models that are well made, and they check them regularly to make sure they stay safe.

When you are choosing and using your own equipment, you will be responsible for its safety.

Over 2000 people are killed or injured in their own homes every year because of electrical equipment. Some of these deaths or injuries are the result of electric shocks; most of them happen because an electrical fault has started a fire.

Some of the commonest causes of electrical accidents are damaged or wrongly-wired plugs, incorrect fuses, and damaged flexes.

Most of the information you have collected about electrical safety is very general. It has been designed to help people with most of the appliances they might have in their homes. Read it through carefully and sort out everything that refers to equipment you might use for textiles. What other causes of electrical accidents could you add to those above?

Safe arrangements

However carefully your equipment has been chosen and cared for, it can still cause accidents if it is in the wrong place.

Figure 106 shows a room with numerous danger points. Figure 107 is a scale plan of the same room. Trace or copy this and mark on it where you would place everything to make it safe.

Figure 106

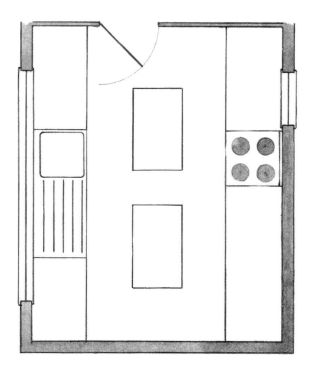

Figure 107

Safe behaviour

A well-organised working area can still be dangerous if people use it carelessly. Have you ever been guilty of any of the bad habits in figure 108?

Safe textiles

The biggest danger with textiles is fire. If you have ever been splashed with boiling water, you will know how painful it is – not just at the time, but for a long while afterwards. Can you imagine what it would feel like if your clothes caught fire?

Fact   Some fibres are more flammable than others. (Find out which from the *Properties of fibres* chart on page 148.)

Fact   Although new flame-retardant man-made fibres are being developed, they are expensive.

Fact   Nobody has yet developed a really effective flame-resistant finish for other textiles (see pages 110–111).

Fact   Fire needs air to help it burn.

Fact   Hairy yarns trap more air than smooth yarns.

Fact   Loosely woven or knitted fabrics trap more air than tightly made fabrics. So do fabrics with a brushed, nap or pile construction.

Therefore, fabrics and yarns that trap air will be most flammable.

Figure 108 Some dangerous habits.

Figure 109

Figure 110

Figure 111 (a)

(b)

Use the flammability test (see page 175) to find out if this is true. You could either test fabric samples made from the same fibres, but constructed in different ways, or (if you find it difficult to collect enough different fabrics) use several samples cut from the same piece of fabric. Increase the amount of air in each sample by brushing it, or by removing a different number of threads from each one. To reduce the amount of air, twist the sample tightly.

What do you think would be the safest fibre, and type of fabric for each of the people in figures 109, 110 and 111?

Safe design

In industry very few accidents should be caused by textiles these days, because the Health and Safety at Work regulations give very clear guidelines about the type of clothing that should be worn. But there are very few safety regulations about the textiles we use in our daily lives.

It would be tragic if someone was injured, or even killed, because of something you had designed or chosen. Young children and elderly people are most at risk, but accidents can happen at any age (figure 112).

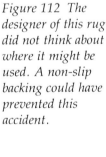

Figure 112 The designer of this rug did not think about where it might be used. A non-slip backing could have prevented this accident.

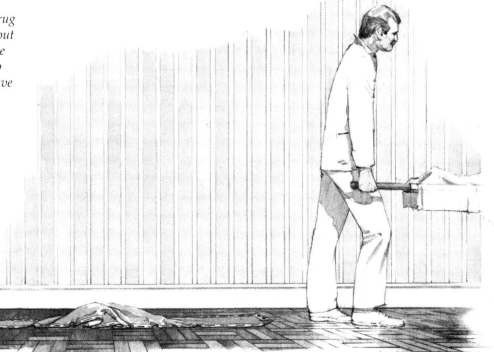

When you are choosing or designing something made from textiles, try to imagine it being used. If it has any parts that trail, dangle or flare out:

is there a risk that these might get caught up in moving machinery, or brush against a naked flame?

would a small child find them attractive? What would happen if he or she tugged at them?

is there a risk that it might get caught on something and cause a bad fall, or knock something over?

Could you do something to make other people more aware of safety with textiles?

You could design a booklet or poster giving advice about choosing and using textile equipment more safely. Or you could design an exhibition, using posters, booklets, and real items to show the right and wrong way of doing things. (Ask your Trading Standards Officer to lend you some examples from his "chamber of horrors".)

SEE ALSO

Children for ideas when designing textile items.
Equipment for help with choosing, using and caring for equipment.
Instructions for help with using instructions.
Rights and responsibilities for consumer information.
Tests for help with testing the safety of textiles.

Workrooms, by Peter Matthews (Design Centre).
Safety and Security in the Home by Barty, White and Burrel (Design Centre).
Making the Most of Children's Rooms, by Mary Gilliatt (Orbis for Marks & Spencer).

Shops

Collect leaflets about savings and credit schemes, from post offices, banks, building societies, shops and mail-order firms.

In order to compete with their rivals, retailers have to find out as much as they can about their market sector, and do everything they can to make the people in that sector want to buy from them rather than other shops.

Here is how one fashion retailer sees her market.

"We have one small shop just off the high street of a busy town . . . The majority of our customers are in the 25 to 55 age group and have good jobs, or run their own businesses. They want clothes that are unusual but not a one-season-wonder. Stylish but well made. They want personal service, advice and inspiration, and they are prepared to pay for it . . ."

(Fashion Weekly, 22.1.87)

Are there any shops like this near you?

How do you think a fashion retailer would describe customers in *your* market sector?

In most towns there will be more than one shop aiming at the same market sector. Competition between them is very tough indeed.

"Many retailers have now realised that investment in up-to-the-minute displays cannot only improve their image, but also raise sales . . . the fashion-conscious shopper is more likely to walk through the doors of a design-conscious retailer."

(Fashion Weekly, 22.1.87)

You may have noticed how, if one firm changes its image, most of the others will begin to change theirs, too. Millions of pounds can be spent on these "face-lifts".

Mail-order companies, and retailers who aim at a very specialised market (such as sewing equipment, or craft materials) do not usually have this sort of competition on their doorstep but they still have to attract customers.

Collect some adverts for mail-order companies, and some of their catalogues. Visit some specialist shops. How do they try to persuade people to buy from them?

With a group of friends, think about the places where you can buy clothes, fabrics and patterns, furnishings, yarns and other craft materials, haberdashery, tools, and textile equipment. Make a list of the shops or catalogues you and your friends like best for buying these items, and discuss the reasons.

The reasons may be different for different goods. For example, you might like a certain clothes shop because of the way the goods are laid out, or a craft shop because it stocks unusual items or the assistants are helpful.

Carry out a survey to find out where and how other people like to buy things, and why. You could interview people of widely varying ages and life styles.

Are you a successful shopper?

Think about some of the things made from textiles or craft materials you have bought during the past year. Did you make any dreadful mistakes? What were your best buys?

Bring some of them to school and tell your class about them: where you bought them, why you chose them, and when you realised that each of them was a good or a bad buy.

If you could go back in time, what advice would have helped you to avoid making the mistakes?

Find out about other people's best and worst textile or craft buys. Ask some of your teachers, and other adults in your family or near where you live. Ask them what advice they would give, to stop other people making the same mistakes.

What makes a good shopper?

Here are some people's ideas – do you agree with them?

Expert shoppers never buy anything that they haven't thought about first - they never buy on impulse.

They know exactly what they're looking for.

They buy second-hand goods whenever they can.

They always seem to know where you can get bargains.

They'll sometimes spend weeks gathering information - visiting lots of shops to look at the goods and compare prices, and reading magazines like <u>Which</u>.

They never buy anything without trying it on or trying it out first.

They always examine things very carefully- read all the information on the label and then look at every little detail on the thing itself.

They know all about guarantees and their rights as customers.

They know exactly how much they can afford to spend and never go over that amount.

If something's not right, they never just put up with it - they go straight back and complain.

Good shoppers sometimes make mistakes, but they never make the same mistake twice.

Discuss the ideas above with a group of friends, and then write out your own list of Rules for Good Shopping.

With your Rules in mind, what advice would you give to someone about buying:

a jacket for him or herself,

a sweater for a friend's birthday present,

a sewing machine,

materials for a wall-hanging,

curtains for his or her bedroom.

How will you pay?

Shops and banks are not allowed to give you credit until you are 18. So you probably don't have much choice now about how you pay for things. But when you do have a choice, how will you decide (figure 113)? Will you save up and pay cash (which will mean going without things *before-hand*), or will you buy it on credit (which will mean going without things *later*)?

If you can, read the section on Credit in the book *Home and Consumer* in this series, and then discuss the advantages and disadvantages of these two methods of paying.

Why do you think so many people seem to get into trouble with buying on credit?

Figure 113 Two views on credit.

> I don't like the idea of being in debt, and anyway it costs more. If I can't afford to pay cash, I'll either save up for it or go without.

> That's ridiculous - you don't think twice about buying a house or a car on credit, so what's so awful about buying clothes and furnishings that way as well? And anyway, by the time you've saved up, the price has probably gone up as well, so you're not really any better off.

> Just you wait - you'll find you're still shelling out good money for things you stopped using months ago. I know - it happened to me once, with a winter coat.

Budgeting

In 1987 the average household in Great Britain spent about one-fifth of its income on food, and just over one-twentieth of its income on clothing and footwear.

When you draw up a budget (you will find help with this in the book *Home and Consumer* in this series), how much do you allow for things like clothes or craft materials? Compare notes with some of your friends: how high up do these things come on your lists of priorities? Do you really know how much of your income you spend on them in a month, or a year?

When you have a home of your own, will your priorities be the same as they are now? Or will they be more like those of the average family (see above)?

SEE ALSO

Advertising for information about how people try to persuade you to buy their goods or services.
Rights and responsibilities for consumer information.

The book *Home and Consumer* in this series: Budgeting, Credit, and Shopping topics.
The Bargain Book (How not to pay the full retail price for almost anything) by Barty Phillips, Pan Books, 1982.

Tests

Collect some fabric samples. (Other items you need are listed at the beginning of each test.)

When you are working with textiles you have to make a lot of decisions, about methods, materials, and equipment. In order to make these decisions you need information; tests are one of the ways in which you can get it.

Designing your own tests

First, decide exactly what it is you want to find out. For example, a new screen-printing ink has just come on to the market, and you want to compare it with the one you have been using. You might decide to compare:
how well the inks perform on different fabrics; or
how easy they are to fix; or
how fast the colours are.

If your test is going to give you useful information it is important that it is a *fair test*.

It would not be fair if you tested the old ink on fabrics made from cotton, nylon and silk, and tested the new ink on polyester, hessian and acrylic. Would it be fair if you used a photographic screen for one ink, and a torn-paper stencil for the other? Would it be fair if you followed the fixing instructions for one ink exactly, and were not so careful with the other? Would it be fair if you washed the samples separately?

Try to make sure that your tests only have one *variable*. (That means, everything must be exactly the same, with only one difference.)

If you look at the shrinkage test on page 170 you will notice that the samples are the same size; they are marked with the same sized squares; they are all put into the same pan of water, for the same length of time. The only difference (the variable) is the fabrics.

If your test is going to change a fabric or yarn in some way (dyeing, washing, pleating, gathering), keep a sample of it in its original state, for comparison. (This is called a *control*.)

If time, temperature, size or weight are important, measure them very accurately.

Record your results carefully. You will find it helps if you have prepared a results sheet beforehand.

Designing tests is not easy. You may find that you have to try out a new test, and change it in a variety of ways, before you are satisfied that it is really accurate and fair.

On the following pages are some tests you may find useful. While you are doing them, think about any ways they could be improved.

To find out how well a fabric performs

Most of these tests will help you to decide which of several fabrics will do a particular job best. But you can, of course, use them to find out about a single fabric as well. If you are testing more than one fabric, make sure that it is a fair test: treat every fabric exactly the same – the only thing that should be different is the type of fabric.

Will it crease? How quickly will creases drop out?

You want to know if the fabric is *crease-resistant* and if it is *resilient*.

Test (a)
1) Crush the fabric in your hand for ten seconds and then let it go.
2) Did the fabric lie crumpled in your hand, or did it spring back into shape?
3) Shake the fabric and smooth it out. How creased is it now?

Fabrics used for clothing are often crushed much harder than this, and for much longer. The next test is much more realistic because as well as your body-heat it uses your weight.

Test (b)
1) Crush a sample of each fabric (about 10 cm × 10 cm) and sandwich them between two sheets of paper or thin card.
2) Sit on them for at least 10 minutes while you get on with something else (making a chart like the one in figure 114?)
3) Hang the chart up and fix the samples to it. Make sure that the top of each sample is exactly level with the top line.
4) Mark on the chart in figure 114 exactly where the bottom of each sample comes
(i)   as soon as you hang them up;
(ii)   after an hour;
(iii) after a day.

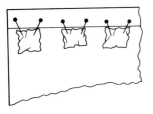

Figure 114 Chart for crease-resistance test.

Will it shrink?

You may want to know about fabrics that will have to be washed.

Test (a)
You will need:
indelible pen (a laundry marker is ideal) or a needle and pale thread;
pan of water and something to heat it on;
paper towels; ruler; iron.

1) Cut samples of each fabric 12 cm square.
(If you know which way the warp yarns run, mark this with an arrow.)
2) Use the indelible pen to mark a 10 cm square in the middle of each sample. (If this won't show up on dark fabrics, mark the square with a row of fairly short tacking stitches, making them cross at the corners.)

Safety note:
Take care not to scald
yourself.

3) Put the samples in a pan of water and gradually bring it to the boil
4) Pour off the boiling water and refill the pan with cold water.
5) Blot the samples with paper towels and smooth them out flat.
6) Measure the marked squares.
7) Iron the samples until they are smooth and dry, then measure the marked squares again.

Alternatively you may be working with a fabric that is not washable, but will need to be damp pressed.

Test (b)
You will need:
indelible pen or needle and thread;
damp cloth and iron for pressing.

1) Cut and mark samples as before.
2) Press each sample using a damp pressing cloth and a hot iron.
3) When the sample is quite dry, measure the marked square.

If a sample has shrunk, notice whether this has happened more along the warp or weft threads.

Will it wear out?

You want to find out how well a fabric *resists abrasion*.

Test (a)
You will need:
a sheet of sandpaper (fine grade);
a block of wood (about 25 cm × 7 cm × 7 cm);
some drawing pins.

1) Fix the sandpaper firmly to a flat surface.
2) Wrap the fabric sample tightly round the block of wood and fix it in place with the drawing pins.
3) Rub the fabric backwards and forward across the sandpaper, counting each rub.
4) After every ten or twenty rubs, examine the fabrics and make a note of their condition.

Notes: This test can be quite tiring. You may find it helps to do it in pairs, or in small groups.
Because there is no way of telling whether you are pressing harder with some samples than with others, this cannot be called a really fair test. It can only be a very rough guide.

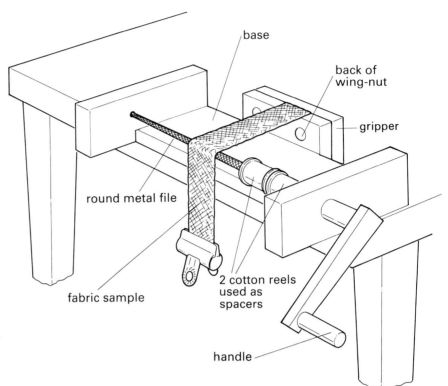

Figure 115 Diagram of abrasion tester.

It is quicker, fairer and less tiring to use a simple home-made abrasion tester.

Test (b)
You will need:
an abrasion tester (see figure 115);
a 200 g weight in a cloth bag ⎱ or a bulldog clip
a stapler. ⎰

1) Cut a strip of fabric exactly 20 cm × 3 cm.
2) Mark a line exactly 3 cm in from one end.
3) Unscrew the wing-nuts at the back of the tester and put the marked end of the fabric in the gripper. The line you marked should just show.
4) Screw the wing-nuts up tight. (If the fabric is too thin to be gripped firmly, try padding it with a 3 cm square of thicker cloth.)
5) Move the abrasion tester to the edge of the table.
6) Staple the bag containing the weight to the end of the fabric strip or put the bulldog clip on the end of it.
7) Drape the fabric over the file and let it hang down. (Make sure it doesn't touch the table.)
8) Ask a partner to hold the tester steady while you turn the handle, counting every turn.
9) Notice when the fabric starts to show signs of wear.
10) Keep turning (and counting) until the fabric breaks.

Will it keep people warm?

You want to find out if the fabric (or padding) is a *good insulator*.

You will need:
a thermometer (a jam thermometer will do very well);
something in which to heat water;
something (a cocoa-tin or a plastic beaker) to hold hot water. Note: try to find something fairly small for this – large containers will need very large samples for the test.
a stop-clock, or stop-watch.

Safety note: take care with boiling water and the hot container.

1) Boil some water.
2) Half fill the container with hot water and take its temperature. Make a note of this, and start the stop-clock.
3) Note how long it take for the temperature to drop 30 degrees. (This will be between 5 and 10 minutes, depending on the temperature of the room.)
4) Repeat steps 1, 2 and 3 exactly, but this time give the container a "jacket" of the material you are testing.

How much longer does it take for the temperature of the water to drop 30 degrees?

Will it keep people warm in windy weather?

You can adapt the insulation test for this.

You will need:
all the equipment for the insulation test;
a hair-dryer or fan that can blow cold as well as hot.

Carry out the insulation test, but blow cold air on to the water container while it is cooling. Note: Keep the fan exactly the same distance away from the water container for each fabric you test.

Will it blot up water or perspiration?

You want to know how *absorbent* the fabric is.

Test (a)
You will need:
an eye-dropper full of water;
a metal or plastic tray.

1) Place a fabric sample on the tray.
2) Hold the eye-dropper 10 cm above the fabric.
3) Gently squeeze out a drop of water and let it fall on to the middle of the fabric sample.

4) Watch what happens. Does the water:
a) immediately soak into the fabric?
b) sit on the surface for a while and then gradually soak in?
c) stay sitting on the surface, like a flattened ball?

Test (b)
You will need:
some very accurate scales (you may need to borrow these from the
Science Department);
some empty yogurt pots;
a bowl of water.

1) Cut all your samples of fabric to exactly the same size.
2) Put a sample in a yogurt pot and weigh it.
3) Pick up the sample by two corners.
4) Dip it in the bowl of water, making sure that all of it is under water.
5) Keep it there for exactly 5 seconds.
6) Lift it out, hold it above the bowl for exactly 30 seconds and let it
drip.
7) Give it a gentle shake, then replace it in the yogurt pot. Weigh it
again.
8) Take the original (dry) weight of the fabric from this (wet) weight to
find out how much water the fabric has absorbed.
Note: although all your fabric samples were the same size, they may
not all have been the same thickness. Can you think of a way of
allowing for this, and therefore making the test fairer?

It would be interesting to repeat the tests using warm water.

Will it keep things dry?

You want to find out how *waterproof* or *water-repellant* the fabric is.

Test (a)
Repeat absorbency test (a) with these differences:

1) Fill the eye-dropper with a *coloured* liquid;
2) Put a sheet of plain white kitchen paper under the fabric sample;
3) Note how much liquid has soaked through on to the kitchen paper.

Test (b)
You will need:
one or more jam-jars (all exactly the same size)
rubber bands;
a bath shower, or a watering-can with a fine rose.

1) Stretch a fabric sample tightly over the top of a jam-jar and hold it in
place with a rubber band.
2) Stand the jam-jar in a sink or large basin.

3) Spray water over the jam-jar for exactly ten seconds (keep the spray head about 30 cm above the top of the jam-jar).

4) Examine the fabrics. Mark the water level in the jam-jar.

5) Repeat steps 3 and 4 four more times.

What if it catches fire?

Safety note: burning fabrics can be very dangerous. To do this test safely it is worth while making a flammability tester (see figure 116). In any case, take great care, wear goggles throughout and follow all instructions exactly.

You want to find out if the fabric is *flammable, flame-resistant* or *flame-retardant.*

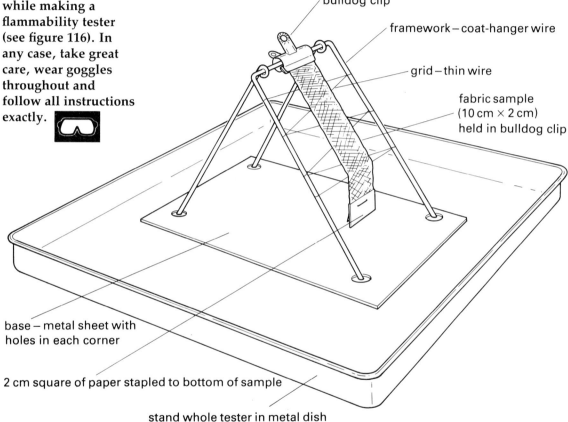

bulldog clip

framework – coat-hanger wire

grid – thin wire

fabric sample (10 cm × 2 cm) held in bulldog clip

base – metal sheet with holes in each corner

2 cm square of paper stapled to bottom of sample

stand whole tester in metal dish

Figure 116 Diagram of flammability tester.

You will need:
flammability tester
goggles for eye protection;
a metal tray;
a box of matches and a taper;
a stop-clock or stop-watch;
some paper, a ruler and some scissors;
a stapler.

1) Cut a strip of your fabric exactly 10 cm × 2 cm.
2) Cut a strip of paper exactly 2 cm square.
3) Staple the paper to one end of the fabric; *they should overlap by 1 cm.*
4) Grip the other end of the fabric in the bulldog clip.
5) Lay the fabric over the wire grid, letting the last 2 cm (the end with the paper) hang straight down.
6) Set the stop-watch to zero and light the bottom of the paper. As it burns it will turn black.
7) As soon as the black reaches the bottom of the fabric, *start timing.*
8) Stop the watch when the fabric stops burning.

If you are using this test to evaluate fabrics for clothing, put a sheet of polythene on the tray under the fabric. When you have finished the test, examine the polythene. It will give you an idea of what would happen to human skin.

To find out what a fabric or yarn is made from

Note: these tests work well with untreated yarns and fabrics that have been made from a single type of fibre. However, they are not so reliable if the yarn or fabric contains a mixture of fibres, or has had something added to it (dyes, printing inks, a special finish).

The only really certain way to find out what a fabric or yarn is made from is to read the label.

Try to practise the tests first with natural (undyed) fabrics or yarns, where you already know the fibre content. If you have problems finding fabrics like this, the Shirley Institute (address on page 200) sells sets of fabrics made from a range of natural and man-made fibres.

When you are used to carrying out the test, and know what to expect, see what sort of results you get when the fabrics or yarns have been coloured in some way, or contain a (known) mixture of different fibres.

If you are testing a woven fabric, pull out some threads and test these. Test warp and weft yarns separately – they may be different.

If you are testing a fancy yarn, untwist it and test the *ground, effect* and *binder yarns* separately. (See page 194 to find out what these terms mean.)

If you can, examine the fibres under a microscope first, and compare them with the photographs in figures 59, 64, 67, 69 and 71. As you can see, some fibres are easy to recognise, particularly wool and cotton. If you are still not sure, or if you want to check that you are right, the next step is to carry out a burning test.

The burning test

You will need:
goggles for eye protection;
a metal tray;
a pair of metal tongs or tweezers;
matches or a long taper.

1) Use the tongs or tweezers to hold *small* (1 cm) samples of the yarn or the fibres horizontally over the metal tray.
2) Light the taper, and *very slowly* move it towards the end of the yarn. Watch the end of the yarn carefully *all the time* – something may happen before the flame actually touches it.
3) Once the flame has touched the yarn, take it away and go on watching.
4) Sniff gently and cautiously, to see if any smell is given off. The smell given off by the burning fibres is an important part of this test. Sniff some vinegar and some celery, and burn some hair, grass and paper so you know what they smell like.

Figure 117 Results of burning tests for the main fibres.

	As it gets near the flame	When it touches the flame	After it has touched the flame	Smell	Residue (What is left after the test)
Protein fibres: wool silk	fibres stick together and curl away from the flame	burn very slowly	stop burning	like burning hair, feathers or nail-clippings	black ash- easy to crush
Cellulosic fibres: cotton linen viscose	—	burn quickly	go on burning	like burning paper	grey ash, like sheet of thin paper
Polyamides	fibres melt and shrink away from the flame; may drip	melt and burn slowly	usually go out	like celery	hard bead – light grey or beige
Polyesters	melt and shrink away from flame	melt and burn slowly: black smoke produced	usually go out	strong, unpleasant, sweetish	hard uncrushable bead
Acrylics	fibres stick together and shrink away from the flame	burn and melt	go on burning and melting	—	hard black bead – rather brittle
Acetates	fibres stick together and shrink away from the flame	burn and melt	go on burning and melting	vinegar and burned paper	hard black bead; shiny

5) When it has had time to cool off, examine what is left of the yarn. What does it look like? What does it feel like? What happens if you squash it?

6) Compare your results with figure 117.

Shirlastains

Your teacher can buy these from the Shirley Institute (address on page 200). Full instructions are provided with the stains. They are a very accurate way of testing for fibre content but, like the burning test, they are only really reliable on pure, untreated fabrics.

SEE ALSO

Design
Exams
Finishing fabrics
Introduction
Research and investigation to see where tests may be needed with your work.
Safety

KEY WORD

Control a sample of material that is to be tested (used for comparison to see whether the test has caused any changes).

Trade names and generic names

When you read the section on man-made fibres (pages 133–40), you will notice that each fibre seems to have several names.

One name describes what the fibre is made from or how it is made. This is the fibre's *generic name*, and it always starts with a small letter. But the fibre will be made and sold by lots of different firms, all over the world. Each firm will make up a special name for the fibre it sells. These are the fibre's *trade names*, and they always start with a capital letter.

Figure 118

For example, the generic name for the liquid we use for cleaning the dishes is "washing-up liquid". Lots of firms around the world make and sell washing-up liquid, and they each give it their own trade name, like Fairy Liquid or Sunlight.

Here are the names of some fibres:

acetate acrilan acrylic agilon antron arnel astralene astralon ban-lon bemberg blue C nylon bri-nylon celafibre celafil celon chlorofibre courlene cournova courpleta courtelle courtolon creslan crimplene crylor cuprama cuprammonium cupresa dacron dicel diolen dralon dynel enkalene enkalon enkona evlan fibreglass fibro fluflene fluflon fortisan fortrel glass-fibre helanca kodel lancola lanon lansil leacril lirelle lycra meraklon modacrylic nylfrance nylon orlon polyamide polyester polyethylene polypropylene qiana rayonne rhodia rhonel saran sarille teklan tergal terlenka terylene trevira tricel tricelon ulstron viloft vincel viscose vycron.

Which are generic and which are trade names? Look through the section on man-made fibres, and use your reference books to help you sort out which is which. Then make a table, matching up the trade names with their generic names. For example:

Generic name	Trade name
acetate	Rhodia, . . .

Woven fabrics

Collect some fabric scraps and an assortment of yarns; a magnifying glass: and small (about 6 cm × 10 cm) pieces of card.

Woven fabrics have always been made on some kind of loom. If you look into the history of weaving, or read about weaving in developing countries, you will discover that wonderful fabrics can be woven on very primitive looms. Their only disadvantage is that they are very slow. Modern mass-produced fabrics are made on sophisticated power-driven looms, which can weave over 18 weft yarns a second. Very simplified, a modern loom looks like figure 119.

Figure 119 Simplified diagram of a modern loom.

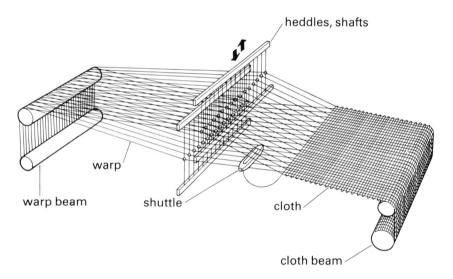

heddles, shafts

warp

warp beam

shuttle

cloth

cloth beam

Some facts about woven fabrics

- There are three basic weaves: plain weave, satin weave and twill weave.
- To make a woven fabric you need at least two sets of yarns. These are called the **warp** and the **weft** yarns.
- Woven fabrics stretch most on the bias (diagonally). They stretch least along the warp threads (the straight grain).
- Thousands of different woven fabrics can be made by changing one or more of the following factors:

1) the fibres;
2) the yarns;
3) the spacing of warp and weft yarns (the *thread count*);
4) the order in which the warp and weft threads cross each other;
5) special finishing treatments;
6) printing or dyeing.

You will find it easiest to understand how (2) and (3) affect the fabric if you weave some small samples yourself. To save time, you could do this in a group and make one or more samples each. While you are working, compare notes with one another about how easy each method is.

Use a small piece of card (7 or 8 cm square) for each sample. Wind yarn round each card to make a warp. Make the cards different, by using thick, medium and thin yarn, and varying the spacing between the warp yarns, as in figure 120.

Figure 120

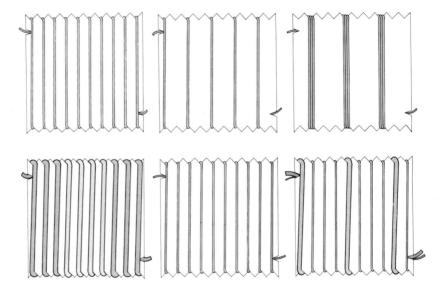

Fasten both ends of the yarns securely. Choose a yarn for your weft; it will need to be quite long. If you find it gets tangled up, you may find it helpful to wind it on to a small offcut of card – in real weaving this would be called a shuttle.

Figure 121 shows you how to do the weaving.

When you have reached half-way up the card, change to a different weft yarn. Choose one that is thicker, or thinner, or a different texture to the thread you have been using, but the same colour if possible. Carry on weaving with this until you run out of space.

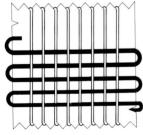

Figure 121 Diagram of plain weave.

Figure 122 Close-up of a selvedge woven on a shuttleless loom.

When you have finished all the samples, examine them carefully, close up and from a distance. How many different fabrics have you managed to make? If you had the time, how many more different fabrics do you think you could make, just by changing the type of yarns and their spacing?

Selvedges

Look at the selvedges on your weaving samples. They will not fray because you have been weaving in the traditional way, with a long weft thread wound on a shuttle. Most of the woven fabrics you use will probably have selvedges like this.

However, many manufacturers are gradually changing over to new types of looms that do not use a shuttle. They are called shuttleless looms. You can recognise fabrics made on them because the selvedges look like those in figure 122.

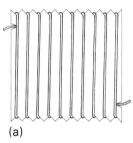

(a)

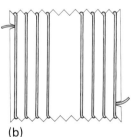

(b)

Figure 123

To understand the difference, make two extra cards, like those in figure 123. For weaving on these cards, do not turn round at the end of each row. Instead, cut off the spare weft thread.

When you have finished, if you cut the fabric on the card (b) up the middle you will find you have woven two pieces of fabric at once. (This way of making two lengths of fabric at the same time can also be done on a traditional loom, in which case the fabric would have one plain and one fringed selvedge.)

When you have finished, examine the fabrics you have made. What do you think are the advantages and disadvantages of each method, for the manufacturer and for the consumer?

The three basic weaves

Plain weave

This is the weave you used on your weaving cards. Figure 124 shows a home-made sample.
- It is the simplest and therefore the cheapest weave to produce.
- Because of its very plain surface, it makes a good background for printing.
- If it has not been printed, a plain weave fabric will look the same on both sides.
- The warp and weft threads interlace with one another more often than in other weaves, so plain weave fabrics are more likely to crease.

Figure 124 Example of a balanced plain weave. This is the simplest type, with the warp and weft yarns the same thickness and spaced the same distance apart.

- For the same reason, a plain weave fabric will not drape as well as a fabric made from the same yarn, but in another weave.
- Depending on the fibres and yarns it is made from, a plain weave fabric will be fairly hard-wearing, though not as hard-wearing as a twill weave.
- Plain weave fabrics can be very fine, medium or thick, depending on the type of yarn used.
- Fabrics made in plain weave can be stiff or soft, depending on how closely the warp and weft threads are packed together.

Figure 125 shows two different plain weaves.

Figure 125 Two plain weave fabrics.

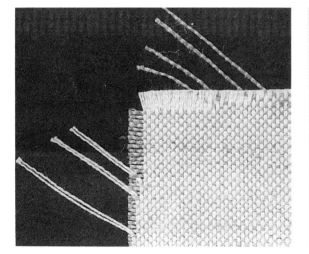

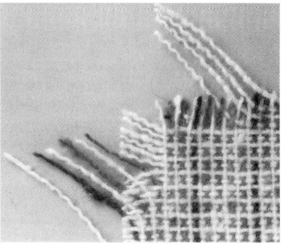

Twill weave

Figure 126 A simple home-made 3/1 twill weave fabric.

Figure 126 shows a sample of twill weave fabric.

If you look carefully, you will see that the weaving pattern moves over to the left on every row. That is what gives twill fabrics their slanting lines, known as **wales**.

Some facts about twill weave

● It is the hardest-wearing weave (which is why your jeans are made in it).

● Because it is more complicated, it can cost more than plain weave.

● The wales always run in the same direction, whichever way up you hold the fabric.

● Twill fabrics have a right and a wrong side. If you examine some, you will also notice that the wales run in the opposite direction on the front and back of the fabric.

● Because they have an uneven surface, twill fabrics show the dirt less than plain weave fabrics.

● The warp and weft yarns do not interlace as often as in a plain weave. Therefore

a) the fabric is not so likely to wrinkle,

Figure 127
(a) The weave here goes over 2 and under 3 (a 3/2 twill).
(b) Here the weave goes over 1 and under 2 (a 2/1 twill).

(a)   (b)

b) the threads can be packed much closer together, making a firmer fabric,

c) the fabric will be more likely to fray.

• The thickness of the wale can be changed by altering the weaving pattern. Figure 126 shows a simple 3/1 twill (which means that the weft thread goes under three warps and over one). Figure 127 shows different weaving patterns.

• The angle of the wale can be altered by varying the spacing of the warp and weft yarns.

• There are more variations possible with twill than with the other two basic weaves. Figure 128 shows some more.

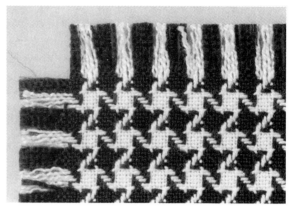

Figure 128

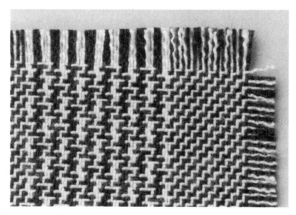

Satin weave

Figure 129 shows a sample of satin weave fabric. The weaving pattern is as follows:

row 1 – under 5	over 1	under 5	over 1	under 5,		
row 2 – under 4	over 1	under 5	over 1	under 5	over 1,	
row 3 – under 3	over 1	under 5	over 1	under 5	over 1	under ⌐
row 4 – under 2	over 1	under 5	over 1	under 5	over 1	under ⌐

Figure 129 A home-made satin weave fabric.

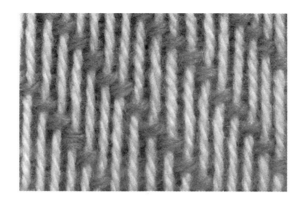

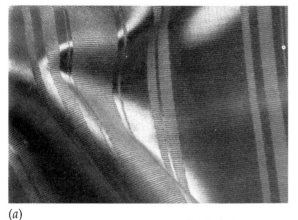

(a)

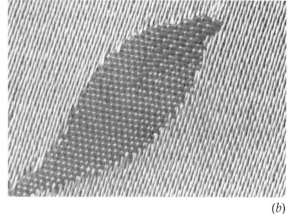

(b)

(c)

Figure 130 A selection of satin weaves.

Some facts about satin weave
- It makes the smoothest fabrics because
a) the warp yarns are set closer together than the weft yarns, and
b) the weft yarns are almost completely hidden by the warp yarns which "float" over them.
- Because the threads do not interlace very often, satin weave fabrics tend to fray easily.
- Satin weave fabrics usually have a right and a wrong side.

- The shiniest satins are made from filament yarns.
- The long floating yarns will snag easily, so satin weaves are not so hard-wearing as plain or twill weaves.
- If the yarns are set close together (high count), the fabric will be stronger, stiffer, more likely to wrinkle, and probably more expensive.
- A low count fabric will be softer, less likely to wrinkle, less hard-wearing and probably less expensive.
- There are not many variations possible with satin weave; figure 130 shows some of them.

Pile fabrics

Figure 131 shows a pile fabric, but the best way to understand how pile fabrics are made is to make some yourself.

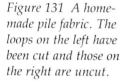

Figure 131 A home-made pile fabric. The loops on the left have been cut and those on the right are uncut.

1) Warp up a small weaving card, as shown in figure 120.
2) Use two different coloured weft yarns, A and B.
3) Work about 6 rows of plain weave in yarn A, beating each row back firmly.
4) Change to colour B, and work one row, pulling the yarn up into a loop as it passes over each warp thread. (You can see how this is done in figure 131. The loops in this piece of weaving are about 1 cm long.)
5) Change to colour A and work a row of plain weave.
6) Change to colour B and work a row of loops.
7) Carry on like this until your fabric is 5 or 6 cm long.

You can now decide whether to leave your fabric as it is (a looped pile fabric), or to cut the loops (a cut pile fabric). You can create a pattern by cutting some of the loops and leaving others uncut. Or you could make a sculptured pile fabric by trimming the pile shorter in some places.

There are many different ways of making pile fabrics. The method you have used is one of the simplest.

Some facts about pile fabrics

• Velvet, velveteen, corduroy, terry towelling and woven carpets are all pile weaves.

• The threads which hold the pile in place are called the *ground fabric*.

• The ground fabric is not always woven – many pile fabrics have a knitted backing.

• The ridges in corduroy are created in the weave. Stripes of floating yarns run up the fabric; when these are cut, they stand up to form the ridges, or wales (see figure 132).

Figure 132 This is what corduroy looks like when it has just come off the loom. Some of the floating threads have been cut to show how the wales are formed.

• Some velvets are made by the double-cloth method: two fabrics are woven face-to-face, with an extra set of yarns joining them together. When the two layers are cut apart, the extra yarns form the pile.

• Not all pile fabrics are knitted or woven. Many are made by "tufting" – pushing little tufts of yarn or carded fibres into the backing. Tufting is a very quick, cheap way of making pile fabrics. Most of the carpets and fur-fabrics on sale today have been made this way.

SEE ALSO

Fabric construction, choosing fabrics

Textiles: Properties and Behaviour in Clothing, by Edward Miller (B. T. Batsford Ltd)
Textiles by N. Hollen, J Saddler and A L Langford (Collier Macmillan Ltd)
Weaving Without a Loom, by Sarita R Rainey (Davis Publications).
Weaving is for Anyone, by Jean Wilson (Van Nostrand Reinhold).
Spinning and Dyeing the Natural Way, by Ruth A Castino (Evans Bros Ltd, London).

Yarns

Collect samples of different yarns: knitting, weaving and sewing yarns; yarns from unravelled fabric scraps.
Some staple fibre (wool, cotton or hair combed from a pet dog or rabbit).
A pair of carders, or dog-brushes; a magnifying glass or yarn counter (×20); or a low-power microscope.

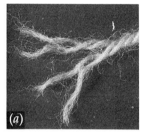

Making fibres into yarn, spinning, is a huge world-wide industry. Some yarns reach us in the form of fabric; some of them are sold in balls, reels or skeins so that the customers can use them for knitting, weaving or other crafts.

The way in which it is made has a very important effect on a yarn and on everything that is made from it. It affects qualities like thickness, colour and texture. It affects properties like insulation, abrasion resistance, crease resistance, absorption, strength and elasticity. The same fibres can be made into yarns that look, feel and behave quite differently, and are therefore suitable for different purposes.

There are three main types of yarn: *Staple, filament* (or multifilament) and *monofilament*. These are shown in **figure 133**.

Staple yarn

Staple yarn, as its name suggests, is made from *staple fibres*, which can be natural or man-made (see page 89).

It is easy to recognise staple yarns, and fabrics that are made from them. Because the fibres are fairly short, there are always some ends sticking out, making the fabric or yarn look rather fuzzy (you may need a magnifying glass to see this in some cases). The shorter the fibres, the more ends there will be to stick out, but how many and how far they stick out will depend on how the yarn was made.

The best way to understand how a staple yarn is made is to make some yourself. Figure 134 tells you how to do this.

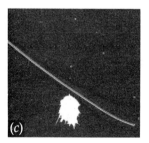

Figure 133 Magnified photographs of the three main types of yarn.
(a) Staple yarn.
(b) Filament or multifilament yarn.
(c) Monofilament.

Figure 134 Hand spinning.

Take a handful of staple fibres and tease them apart with your fingertips until you have a soft, open web.

If you are using natural fibres you may find tiny pieces of straw, twigs or seeds tangled up in them. Remove as much of this rubbish as you can. (If you want to make your yarn from one or more different fibres or colours, you could do it now, see page 144).

If you have a pair of carders or dog-brushes, you can tidy up the fibres by combing them straight. If not, you can make your yarn from the teased-out fibres. It will look and feel slightly different and will be called an *uncarded* yarn.

Now you are ready to spin the yarn; copy figure 134 for this. The first yarns were made like this, thousands of years ago, and the basic idea has not really changed since then.

Tools and equipment have been invented to make spinning much quicker and easier, but all the staple yarns you use have gone through the four stages – cleaning, carding, drawing and twisting – that you have just done. If you need information about yarn production in factories, you will find it in most of your reference books. At first it may seem very complicated. But if you remember the four stages you went through when you made your own yarn, you will find it is much easier to understand.

Did your yarn begin to untwist itself when you let go of it? This is quite usual; the fibres were not used to their new shape, and were trying to get back to normal. Because of this, freshly-spun yarns are often steamed, or kept in a damp place, in order to set the fibres in their new spiral shape.

Strength, thickness and flexibility

Five factors that can make a difference to staple yarn are:
- the *properties* of the fibres from which the yarn is made,
- the length and amount of *crimp* in the fibres,
- the *number of fibres* that are drawn out,
- how *tightly* they are twisted, and
- how carefully the fibres have been *carded*.

Find out about this by making some different yarns. Make them with carded and uncarded fibres. If you can, use some long and some short staple fibres (cotton wool and Kapok wadding have quite short staple lengths.)

Make about 10 cm of yarn from each bunch of fibres. Start by twisting each yarn quite loosely (*soft spun*), then fairly tightly (*hard spun*), then very tightly indeed (*overspun*).

As you make the yarns, notice the differences between them. What do they look like (use a magnifying glass, as well as the naked eye)? What do they feel like? Which yarns are the strongest? The most elastic? Which are the most flexible?

With the help of a friend, arrange the yarns side-by-side and stretch them out straight. Rub them with a hard brush (an old toothbrush would do). Which of them fluffs up most? Which of them loses most fibres? (Examine the brush and see how many fibres are caught in its bristles.)

Which of them do you think would be warmest, most absorbent, best at resisting abrasion, and why?

Filament yarn

This, not surprisingly, is made from filament fibres (see page 89). It should really be called "multifilament yarn", because it is made from more than one filament. The only natural filament yarn is silk. All the rest are man-made.

Filament yarns are much quicker to make than staple yarns. This is because the filaments are almost ready to use as soon as they have coagulated (become solid). All the filaments from one spinneret can be gathered together and twisted into a yarn (see page 138). A spinneret with a lot of holes leads to a thicker yarn than one with a few holes (Figure 135). What difference would using a spinneret with big holes make?

Filament yarns that are made like this are very easy to recognise. Because the filaments are so long, there are no ends that could stick

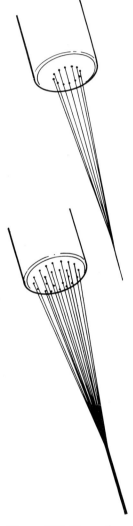

Figure 135 Yarns from spinnerets with different numbers of holes.

out of the yarn. And because the filaments are nearly always smooth and shiny, the fabrics and yarns made from them are smooth and shiny, too.

They are less easy to recognise if the filaments have been textured (see pages 135, 138), but with a magnifying glass you should be able to see whether there are any fibre ends sticking out of the yarn. Twisting filament yarns does not make them any stronger – it simply makes them look less shiny. You can try this out for yourself if you, or someone you know, has very long hair. Take a well-combed strand of their hair and gently pull it straight. Then twist the strand as though you were making a yarn and notice the difference.

Monofilament yarn

A monofilament yarn is made from only one filament. It is always man-made (nylon is the most common) and can be almost any thickness, depending on what it is to be used for.

Monofilament yarns are strong. They are also smooth and springy, which means they can be difficult to make into fabric. You are most likely to find them in lingerie, where the fabric has been made by warp knitting (see page 125).

You may also find monofilament yarns holding up the hems of skirts or trousers. It will have been used because, being almost transparent, it blends in with the colour of the fabric. Manufacturers use these "invisible" monofilaments because it is cheaper and quicker: they don't have to buy stocks of coloured threads, and the machinists can work on different coloured fabrics without having to spend time re-threading their machines.

You will see a thicker monofilament if you look underneath the cutting head of a strimmer, at the bristles in your toothbrush, or at some fishing line

Try using an "invisible" monofilament yarn for hand and for machine stitching. Stitch a seam, and turn up a hem on some different fabrics. Use different tensions and stitch lengths; use straight and zig-zag machine stitches. Finish your samples by pressing them, then do exactly the same using an ordinary sewing thread.

Bearing in mind the price, the quality of the results, and how easy it was to use each type of thread, which do you prefer? When would you use monofilament thread?

Singles, ply and fancy yarns

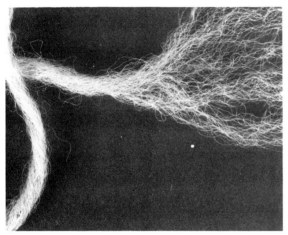

Figure 136 Singles yarn.

Figure 137 (a) 6-ply yarn. (b) 6-cord cable yarn.

When you were making your staple yarns, they may have looked like that in figure 136. This is a *singles yarn*.

If you look through your collection of yarns you will probably find some singles yarns, but you may also find some like those in figure 137. Figure 137(a) shows a *ply* or *folded yarn*. It has been made by twisting six singles yarns together so it is a 6-ply yarn. Figure 137(b) shows a *cable yarn*. It has been made from three 2-ply yarns. This is a 6-cord cable because there are six singles yarns in it.

There are a number of reasons for making ply yarns.

a) They are stronger than singles yarns made from the same fibres.

b) They are more even.

c) They are harder wearing.

d) They are more flexible.

e) Fabric made from them will crease less.

The first four of these reasons are particularly important for sewing thread; why do you think this is?

You may also have found yarns like those in figures 138–139. Figure 138 shows a *core yarn*. The yarn in the centre has been covered by a different fibre spun around it.

Figure 139 shows some *novelty* or *fancy yarns*. The lumps in (a) are called slubs and have been put there on purpose to make an interesting texture. If you look closely at figure 139(b) you can see that there is a strong straight thread (the *ground* yarn), several crinkly threads (the *effect* yarns) and a very thin thread that holds them all together (the *binder* yarn).

As you would imagine, yarns like these are not as hard-wearing as ordinary yarns. Bumps or loops will snag easily. Thick, loosely-twisted

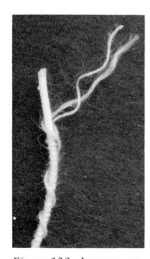

Figure 138 A core yarn.

Figure 139 Fancy yarns.

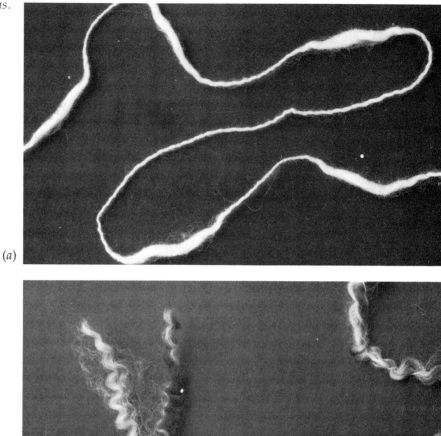

(a)

(b)

portions will first get fuzzy and then wear thin if they are rubbed too much. They are more expensive to produce and can also be more difficult to knit or weave than smooth, even yarns. However, novelty yarns are used a great deal, because of the interesting textures and colour effects that they can create. You can see some examples of novelty yarns in picture 7, between pages 106 and 107.

There are so many different yarns and threads that it is only possible to show you a few of them here. You have seen how, by untwisting a piece of yarn and looking at it carefully, it is possible to discover how it was made. See how many other yarns you can find, and try to work out for yourself how they were made.

Most knitting shops sell a basic range of novelty yarns, which can be very useful for the embroiderer and weaver as well. More unusual yarns can be bought by mail-order from specialist shops. The most interesting yarns, however, can be those you have created yourself.

With a friend (it helps to have someone to hold the end of the yarn) experiment with fibres and ready-made yarns. Here are a few ideas, to start you off.

Twist different textures, colours and thicknesses together.
Cut unusual materials into thin strips and twist them into your yarn.
Make lumps by knotting or twisting unspun fibres into your yarn, or untwisting a plain ply yarn and pushing one of the strands along the others.

In the textile industry terms like 3-ply (or 3-fold) and 4-ply (or 4-fold) mean just what they say. But they do not necessarily mean the same thing when they are used today to describe knitting yarns.

SEE ALSO

Fibres
Fibres from animals⎫ for information about the fibres that yarns
Fibres from plants⎬ are made from.
Man-made fibres⎭

Mixtures and blends for more information about yarns.

Textiles: Properties and Behaviour in Clothing, by Edward Miller (B. T. Batsford Ltd)
Textiles by N. Hollen, J Saddler and A L Langford (Collier Macmillan Ltd)
Weaving Without a Loom, by Sarita R Rainey (Davis Publications).
Weaving is for Anyone, by Jean Wilson (Van Nostrand Reinhold).
Spinning and Dyeing the Natural Way, by Ruth A Castino (Evans Bros Ltd, London).

KEY WORDS
Staple yarn a yarn made from staple fibres.
Filament (or **multifilament**) **yarn** a yarn made from several continuous filaments.
Monofilament a yarn made from a single continuous filament.

Addresses

All the organisations listed below are useful sources of information. The list indicates how they may be able to help but it would be best to telephone first to check any specific requests. It would also be polite to enclose a suitably sized stamped addressed envelope if you write asking for information.

Advertising Standards Authority
15 Ridgmount Street
London WC1E 7AW
(01-580 5555)

Will supply the British Code of Advertising Practice and the British Code of Sales Promotion Practice. Also publishes leaflets on a variety of topics (send for current list) and monthly case reports on firms that have contravened the Codes. All free.

The Advisory Unit
Endymion Road
Hatfield
Herts AL10 8 AU
(07072 65443)

Formerly The Advisory Unit for Computer – based Education. Send for current list of Home Economics related programs.

British Man-made Fibres Federation
24 Buckingham Gate
London SW1E 6LB
(01-828 0744)

Free brochure, with up-to-date inserts on various aspects of man-made fibres. Will also answer specific questions.

British Standards Institution
2 Park Street
London W1A 2BS
(01-629 9000)

British Wool Marketing Board
Oak Mills
Station Road
Clayton
Bradford BD14 6JD
(0274 882091)

Useful leaflets, posters, samples and fleece. Send for current price list.

Chelsea School of Art
Manresa Road
London SW3
(01-351 3844)

Consumers' Association
14 Buckingham Street
London WC2N 6DS
(01-839 1222)

Publishes *Which?* magazine
and books on consumer matters.

Courtaulds Fibres Ltd
PO Box 16
Foleshill Road
Coventry CV6 5AE
(0203 688771)

Design Centre Bookshop
The Design Council
28 Haymarket
London SW1Y 4SU
(01-839 8000)

Send for current catalogue.

Design Council Educational
Freepost
PO Box 10
Wetherby
West Yorks LS23 6YY
(0937 844443)

Sells a variety of teaching and learning
resources dealing with aspects of design. Send
for current list.

DuPont (UK) Ltd
Textile Fibres Department
94 Regent Road
Leicester LE1 7DJ
(0533 470444)

Good Housekeeping Institute
Chestergate House
Vauxhall Bridge Road
London SW1V 1HF
(01-834 2331)

Tests goods and publishes books and leaflets.
Send for current list.

HMSO
P O Box 276
London SW8
(01-622 3316)

The Handweavers Studio and Gallery
29 Haroldstone Road
London E17 7AN
(01-521 2281)

Stocks a very wide range of different yarns and
fibres, and will supply very small quantities.
Also, spinning and weaving equipment. Send
for current catalogue and price list.

Hoechst UK Ltd
Hoechst House
Salisbury Road
Hounslow
Middlesex TW4 6JH
(01-570 7712)

Free folder containing interesting booklet and charts, with samples of polymer chips and different types of Trevira fibres and filaments.

Home Laundering Consultative Council
British Apparel Centre
7 Swallow Place
London W1R 7AA
(01-408 0020)

Provides information about care and labelling of textiles.

ICI Fibres
Hornbeam Park
Hookstone Road
Harrogate
North Yorkshire HG2 8QN
(0423 68021)

International Wool Secretariat
Wool House
Carlton Gardens
London SW1Y 5AE
(01-930 8884)

Free: excellent leaflets on modern textile subjects (not just wool), and well-illustrated brochures on the work of the Secretariat and their Development Centre. Will do their best to answer any specific questions you have.

International Wool Secretariat Development Centre
Valley Drive
Ilkley
Yorkshire LS29 8PB
(0943 601555)

Welcomes visits from individuals or groups. The latest textile processes and machinery can be seen in action.

National Consumer Council
18 Queen Anne's Gate
London SW1H 9AA
(01-930 5752)

N. Ireland Consumer Council
176 Newtownbreda Road
Belfast BT8 4QS
(0232 647151)

Publishes reports on consumer matters. Send for current list.

Scottish Consumer Council
4 Somerset Place
Glasgow G3 7JT
(041-332 3377)

Welsh Consumer Council
8 St Andrews Place
Cardiff CF1 3BE
(0222 25416/27311)

National Federation of Consumer Groups
70–76 Acester Road South
Birmingham B14 7PT
(021-444 6010)

Information about local consumer groups (some publish magazines).

Nottingham Educational Supplies
17 Ludlow Hill Road
Melton Road
West Bridgford
Nottingham NG2 6HD
(0602 234251)

Sells wide range of textile craft materials, including Transfer Printing Inks. Send for latest catalogue.

Office of Fair Trading
Field House
15–25 Bream's Buildings
London EC4 1PR
(01-242 2858)

Send for current list of leaflets.

also at

Hope Street
Edinburgh EH24 4EL
(031-225 3185)

Shirley Institute
Wilmslow Road
Didsbury
Manchester M20 8RX
(061-445 8141)

Sells Shirlastains and samples of fabric for testing. Also publishes *Textiles*, an excellent magazine that comes out three times a year (order from the Publications Office which will also supply details of back numbers available.)

Vilene
68 Hanbury Street
London E1
(01-247 5629)

Worldwide Butterflies Ltd.
and **Lullingstone Silk Farm**
Compton House
Sherborne
Dorset DT9 4QN
(0935 74608)

Supplies silkworm eggs (with instructions), silk samples and other informative material. Send for current price list.

Index

In this index, page numbers followed by "k" refer to keyword definitions